To Gogo

LARS BOLANDER'S
SCANDINAVIAN DESIGN

Skål !!

Lars

LARS BOLANDER'S
SCANDINAVIAN DESIGN

HEATHER SMITH MacISAAC

THE VENDOME PRESS
NEW YORK

CONTENTS

INTRODUCTION

Wood and water, fire and ice, darkness and light—such are the powerful elements of nature that define Scandinavia. If biology is destiny for people, then geography is destiny for countries. Where they sit on the globe determines temperature, topography, resources, and biorhythms—all of which in turn shape how life is lived. Scandinavia, via Denmark, dips onto the European continent, but the northern latitudes it straddles, crossing into the Arctic Circle, have most intensely influenced perceptions of the region.

The hours of darkness, the depths of temperature, the harshness of the weather loom large. Cold not only constricts the senses but also concentrates design. Every architectural move is a team member in conserving energy. To master endless winter one must submit to its demands and embrace the darkness. Shrink the floor plan and the windows, build thick and strong with logs and earth. Tuck into a corner, draw near to the hearth. Pile on the animal skins and woolens, load up on candles, never let the fire go out. Such was the way, by necessity, of Norsemen. Such is the way, by choice, of skiers and ice fishermen and other hearty Scandinavians for whom bracing air is a tonic. But hunkering down and drawing inward is not the route chosen by most.

Scandinavians live for light. Like air itself, it is critical to their well-being and all the more cherished because, for many months, they must make do with very little or none at all. A largely secular people is even willing to turn to a saint to carry it through the shortest day of the year, defying the darkness with the St. Lucia festival of light. The littlest glow, like a firefly, carries disproportionate weight and wonder. All the more reason, then, that midsummer—when daylight in as southern a Scandinavian city as Stockholm can fill nineteen of twenty-four hours—provokes rapture.

Inside Scandinavian houses, no matter the season, it's all summer, all the time. At least that's the image—of rooms suffused with light—that has come to define Nordic interiors. With light this white and pure, Scandinavia must be the first step of the stairway to heaven.

Tailored white slipcovers bring an exquisite 1770s Swedish dining room down to earth.

Certainly, during the long days of brief summers, Scandinavians actively worship the light, doing all they can to eliminate the distinctions between indoors and out. Interiors swell with fresh air and vibrate with sun. Rooms seem to stretch as if to soak up enough of a charge of energy to carry them through the long winters.

If sun is the beacon, nature is the guide. No force has had and still maintains more influence over builders in Scandinavia. She is responsible for a varied topography that in turn shapes Nordic architecture. She supplies the materials and dictates the weather that determines how they will be used. Her success in creating settings at once dramatic, intimate, and primal has been so great that a vast number of Scandinavians own or have access to a house in the country in order to be closer to her.

For centuries nature was the only authority. Right into the early twentieth century, farming remained the primary industry of a lightly populated land. The self-sufficiency that such an occupation—and such isolation—demands meant that Scandinavians built their own houses and furniture, using materials at hand, largely pine, spruce, and juniper. Climatic conditions drove design. With one third of Norway located within the Arctic Circle, temperatures frigid enough to warp marble are not unheard of. And with strong prevailing winds along the coast kicking up steady salt spray, it is no wonder that houses took the form of sturdy sentries, their openings barely a squint. (Together, the Norse words for wind and eye form the English word *window*.)

Log cabins as well constructed and weatherproof as Viking ships benefited from the same pine-tar preservative long used on wooden boats. The inky protective layer turned common houses into iconic structures as artfully severe as shapes in a Richard Serra paintstick drawing. Other dwellings, dwarfed by the landscape yet easy to spot in their brilliant coats of red, blue, or yellow, resemble Lego blocks scattered across the yard. High in the mountains huts batten down, their profile low, their construction solid, amid trees bent horizontal by the winds. Like their seaside brethren built at the foot of sheer stone cliffs, the modest cabins defiantly stake their ground below looming peaks and menacing glaciers.

Like jewels sent through the mail in protective plain brown wrappers, the worn and weathered houses of Norway often deliver a stunning surprise: magical, colorful paintings springing to life on every interior surface. Vivid narratives rooted in local lore and motifs drawn from nature adorn whole walls and rooms, box beds and weighty chests, transporting wood environments to mythical lands. It's as if, as the winter months wear on, the housebound can no longer tolerate confinement and erupt in exuberant expression. The internal life of Norwegians is indeed spirited. This is folk art as bold as the mountains.

If the landscape of Norway is heroic, that of Finland is dreamlike, with light filtering through boundless woods and glancing off infinite lakes and endless sea. The most heavily forested of all European countries, Finland is also home to 190,000 lakes and Europe's largest archipelago. Like forest nymphs, houses of weathered wood peak out from behind rock ledges and tree trunks or disappear altogether. Finns celebrate the graces of nature and accept the challenge of living at one with the elements. Their houses are as rigorous and adaptable as they are visual manifestations of *sisu*, a Finnish term for persistence. When it comes to design, the credo is: make it humble, make it harmonious, and above all, make it work.

Taking its cue from the terrain, Finnish architecture is low profile. Simple, rustic dwellings foster intimate contact with others and with nature, sustaining cultural rituals. Friends and family share modest living and sleeping spaces, bathe in the lake and partake of the

The porcelain kitchen at Thureholm Manor is unrivaled in its wedding of faux painting to a prized collection.

Carolus Linnaeus's private suite of rooms is decoratively alive with his passion for botany.

sauna communally, and fish and ski and berry-pick together. Though colorful summer villas and bathhouses dot the coastline in the south, their bright facades and fanciful detailing are more expressions of Swedish or Russian influence than of homegrown design. Like delicious, organic, handmade granola, Finnish design is a thoughtfully blended amalgam of natural, nourishing elements.

More than the Baltic Sea separates Denmark from the rest of Scandinavia. A peninsula springing from the European continent, the small country has plenty of coastline, but its land is flat and dominated by farms rather than forest. Fields of rye and oat grass traditionally supplied as much thatch for roofs as grain for the table. A milder climate means larger windows have long been part of the architectural vocabulary, opening up interiors early on.

Design in Denmark reflects a pragmatism common to all Scandinavia but less beholden to nature, no doubt because the country is less in her grasp. Houses and castles stand upright and proud, staking a claim to the land instead of becoming one with it.

Tiled-roof dwellings of bricks and stone, often stuccoed or half-timbered, reflect not only the dearth of lumber but the easy spread of stylistic influences from the Continent, particularly Germany to the south. Houses in the Skåne region of southern Sweden—formerly a Danish province—are largely indistinguishable from Danish dwellings.

Of all the Scandinavian countries, Sweden is home to the widest range of domestic architectural styles, from rustic huts and ice palaces in the north to farmhouses in the lake district, summerhouses on islands, manor houses and castles in and around Stockholm, and half-timbered houses in the south. Much of the variety can be attributed to the diversity of topography, climate, and raw materials in a land mass the size of California (with a population of a mere nine million). Sweden has low farmland, high mountains, and an archipelago of islands, expansive forests and extensive coastline, mines and mills, temperate pockets and areas of deep freeze.

Like their Finnish and Norwegian neighbors, Swedes care deeply about the natural environment.

Nothing less than their constitution guarantees the longstanding tradition of *Allemansrätten,* or Right of Public Access, whereby every citizen has the right to roam, on foot, onto anyone's land. Along with access comes the duty to respect fauna and flora: one can bird-watch but not disturb a nest, pick flowers and berries as long as they are not officially protected, gather fallen branches for a fire but light it only when it's safe and never on bare rocks that could crack and split.

The "do not disturb, do not destroy" ethic of *Allemansrätten,* an outgrowth of Scandinavia's rural past, applies as well to design and decoration. Paying close attention to nature has multiple benefits. People who draw their livelihood from the land are good custodians of its resources. Waste is anathema. Frugality, pragmatism, and self-sufficiency are virtues. Craft honors a material's natural properties. Things are made well to last more than one lifetime; rare is the object that is purely decorative. Yet, from such stern and sober stuff emerges a surprisingly light, lighthearted, and refined aesthetic, especially in Sweden.

What accounts for the sophistication that pervades every aspect of design—not just the architecture of a palace but the contours of a tea table and the graphic clarity of a transit map? Seemingly isolated in the northern latitudes, Scandinavia nevertheless has a broad outlook. One can't help but think that an alluring watery horizon, the inescapable accompanist to an endless coastline, is a constant prompt to consider, if not actively explore, what lies beyond. The Vikings didn't just prowl local waters; in their impressive longships they raided settlements as far off as Canada in the west and Constantinople in the east. Perhaps the everyday challenges of living in a demanding environment lower the barriers to striking out on risky ventures. Certainly, living in the dark can make one long for brighter realms.

The Age of Enlightenment that swept Europe in the eighteenth century seized Scandinavia and Sweden in particular like the fireball of a late afternoon sun, penetrating deep into the culture, lighting up dark corners, and launching an examination of the balance between nature and culture that persists still. Enlightenment in Sweden coincided with its own Age of Liberty, a fifty-year period of peace that not only was free from monarchy but freely embraced a parade of styles, helped along by expanded trade, broader travel, and the reach of influential texts and pattern books. Graceful furniture modeled after the work of English cabinetmakers like Hepplewhite and Chippendale supplanted earlier and heavier Dutch- and Flemish-inspired furnishings; Baroque rooms with dark and sober wall paintings gave way to brighter, more lighthearted Rococo rooms.

Swedes imported with a vengeance goods and inspiration not just from the Continent but from farther afield. The Swedish East India Company, founded in 1731, unleashed truly exotic flavors—less of East India than of China—on quiet northern fare. In its eighty-one years of existence, the trading company imported a staggering load of porcelain (an estimated fifty million pieces) from Canton, fueling and satisfying a hunger for chinoiserie, itself imported from the Continent. To keep up with demand and keep kronor at home, Sweden's Rörstrand faience factory, the second-oldest ceramics manufacturer in Europe (established 1720), produced its own version of Chinese-inspired tableware.

Along with porcelain and lacquered furniture, prosperous Swedes imported artisans to transform (and train others to metamorphose) whole rooms into Orientalist and Rococo fantasies, influenced by the current vogue in France. Astonishing rooms and structures emerged: the kitchen at Thureholm, painted so exquisitely as to seamlessly blend with the valuable blue and white Chinese export porcelain it housed; the remarkable Chinese garden pavilion at Drottningholm Palace; the interiors at Åkerö, which capture in masterful trompe l'oeil the period's growing fascination with both the natural and classical worlds.

Raw nature and civilized order: nothing holds greater sway over Swedish style. Though seemingly stylistic opposites, the two spheres dovetail beautifully. And it is two eighteenth-century Swedish figures, neither a designer, who loom largest, even now, especially now, in representing the confluence: Carolus Linnaeus and King Gustav III (reigned 1771–92). Linnaeus's fame grew from his having developed a system—binomial nomenclature—for classifying all living things. But it was Hammarby, his turf-roofed farmhouse near Uppsala, that established a paradigm for Swedish interiors. Given Linnaeus's achievement and prominence, his home's very modesty is ostensibly contradictory yet characteristically Scandinavian.

Hammarby may be humble but it is seminal, a primer of Swedish interior style. Inside, floors and ceilings of planed planks are unadorned. Furniture consists of the essentials, but each piece exhibits a presence and grace. Linnaeus's collection cabinet is a functional masterpiece—a cupboard raised on cabriole legs, its two doors guarding thirty shallow drawers painted a range of soft grays. Interiors are spare with an emphasis on symmetry—of room and furniture arrangement, window placement, wallpaper alignment. All is orderly and calm.

The surprise arrives in Linnaeus's most private retreat, his drawing room and adjacent bedroom. Above a gray-painted dado, the walls are papered to the ceiling with sheets of delicate, hand-colored engravings of plants and flowers—an eloquent rendering of his occupation, his passion, and his heritage. This botanical jewel box of a room, at once subtle and radical, is the root of many an exquisite Scandinavian salon and modest chamber, not to mention hundreds of wallpapers, painted tiles, and floral fabrics from delicate calicos to the bold twentieth-century prints of Josef Frank.

Powerless to resist their bond with nature, Swedes celebrate it, via pattern and detail, elevated craft, and, architecturally, by opening up rooms to capture it. All of these approaches are found in the style named for Sweden's greatest royal patron of the arts, though what comes first to mind in picturing

Gustavian rooms is a cool classicism. Well-schooled in the classical canon by his tutors and travels, Gustav III developed a vision for interiors that still reigns as the height of Swedish style. A room in the Gustavian style features elegant proportions, symmetry, delicately rendered classical detailing, a quiet yet shimmering palette of pale grays and blues, furnishings light in both weight and form, large windows, and strategic mirrors. Everything works toward a common goal: grace and light.

For all its elegance, the Gustavian room is grounded. It is the confident and demure sister to its haughty French sibling—the extravagant salons of palaces like Versailles, which Gustav III appreciated firsthand. Gold and sparkle are used sparingly, as are curtains. Colors are soft, fabrics are matte and, given their setting, even plebeian. The original practice of protecting silk upholstery with cotton coverings evolved into an enduring preference for unpretentious checks and stripes over fancier brocades. Whether it's giving a certain informality to the grandest salons or a subtle formality to modest rooms, Swedish interiors consistently express a devotion to harmony and simplicity.

Even with the arrival of industrialization, the Nordic dedication to nature, craft, and a self-effacing aesthetic remained paramount, indeed blossomed in reaction to the unsettling changes in domestic life that accompanied industry. As early as 1875 Finland established the Finnish Society of Crafts and Design to preserve craft traditions and promote industrial arts. Before the end of the century the Norwegian Society for Home Industry (1891) and the Swedish Handicraft Society (1899) had joined the movement. Even more influential was the release in 1899 of *Ett Hem* (A Home), a book by Swedish artist Carl Larsson that set down in watercolor illustrations a visual guide to a happy family dwelling—charming, colorful rooms animated by playful children, painted furniture, cheery textiles, lamp- and candlelight, and potted flowers. From the liberal application of bright

Carl Larsson's use of red on the interior, as in his family dining room, is still hugely influential.

reds, greens, and yellows to the clever use of built-ins, the Larsson house remains *the* model of an informal, comfortable, and welcoming Swedish home.

Amid the throes of a twentieth-century fascination with man-made materials theretofore foreign to domestic interiors, Scandinavians were steadfast in their devotion to natural materials. In fact, what set Nordic design apart from other mid-century design epicenters, in particular Italy and the U.S., was its loyalty to wood. While designers elsewhere produced radical furnishings in plastic and metal, towering homegrown talent like the Danish furniture designers Finn Juhl and Hans Wegner and Finnish architect Alvar Aalto found new ways to express form in wood. Shortly after Bauhaus architects Marcel Breuer and Ludwig Mies van der Rohe debuted cantilever chairs in tubular steel, Aalto produced a version in bent birch wood, a far greater technical challenge. Finn Juhl's masterful exploration of teak launched a style—Danish Modern—that ironically pegged the non-native wood to Denmark and generated waves of poor imitations that watered down an initially refreshing aesthetic.

Contemporary Nordic architecture follows the same dedication to truth over trend. The walls of glass and open floor plan introduced by the International Style promoted spectacular shifts in domestic living that were wholeheartedly embraced by Scandinavians, especially with the development of double- and triple-glazed glass. Let there be light, not just near the windows but throughout the house! But let there be comfort also. Minimalist should never mean cold. For every plane of white and expanse of glass, there are wood floors and ceilings and furnishings to ground a house. And rare is the modern glass pavilion without a substantial hearth at its core.

As far and wide as Scandinavians ultimately drew and still source inspiration, they always have and will pass design through a humanistic filter. In a Nordic home you will never feel overpowered by scale, suffocated by stuff, or put off by clinical minimalism. You *will* feel utterly at ease: comforted by sensitive proportions, delighted by thoughtful details, calmed by unfussy decorating, and subtly yet profoundly connected to a larger world. If anything is going to supply drama, it will be nature. Because no design feature, no matter how clever or sensitive, can ever trump firelight flickering on faces or an open sky just fading to dusk at midnight.

EXTERIORS

With two-thirds of Scandinavia covered in forest, wood has always been the region's primary building material. Only in southern Sweden and Denmark, where flatter topography lent itself to farming, did half-timbering take hold. Though the Vikings built impressive wood and turf long houses, it is the *hytte* (hut) up in the mountains or clinging to the sides of a fjord that Norwegians hold most dear. Constructed initially of logs, later of planks, the huts were most often left to weather naturally, though sometimes a layer of protective and darkly dramatic pine tar was applied. By nature a robust and sporty people, many Norwegians chose not to update their simple houses with electricity and running water until the late twentieth century, if then. Similarly hardy and outdoorsy, the Finns are happy to heat their waterfront log cabins and saunas only with wood and let their houses weather until they disappear into the landscape.

Though Sweden has its share of natural wood structures, strong color has long set its buildings apart in architectural style and in the landscape itself. The red *stuga,* or country cottage, is an icon and remains an aspiration. Applying Falun red—a pigment originally derived from the copper mines at Falun—to a house was initially a sign of a farmer's prosperity. With their own red house in Sundborn on the outskirts of Falun, artists Carl and Karin Larsson fixed the colorful country house as a model of happy family life in the national psyche.

Besides the twentieth century, when technological advances in systems and materials freed houses to be much more open both visually and functionally, the eighteenth century witnessed the most significant changes in residential architecture. Planed planks supplanted log exteriors, leading to larger, better insulated, and more embellished farmhouses. Among the wealthy, a passion for all things French drove a boom in the construction of Rococo and Gustavian manor houses with formal facades, mansard roofs, taller windows, and plastered exteriors washed in a soft yellow to imitate the sandstone used for châteaux. By example if not by reputation, though, the Scandinavians have a leg up on the French when it comes to a quiet elegance.

The bold geometry of a house by Tham & Videgård Hansson belies its sensitivity to living in the wild. Windbreaks, sun screens, and a plan that shapes sheltered spaces temper the forces of nature.

A WAY WITH WOOD

With a wealth of wood at their fingertips, Scandinavians freely explore all of its properties, demonstrating not just masterful carpentry skills but imaginative applications. Exterior cladding captures a timeline of technical advances and architectural fashion.

OPPOSITE The roofline of a simple nineteenth-century Norwegian fishing hut clad in painted planed boards mimics the mountain of stone looming behind it.

RIGHT In the late 1930s architect Alvar Aalto put wood to every possible use (posts, cladding, door, and door handle) for the entrance to Villa Mairea in Noormarkku, Finland.

BELOW Swedish architect Anders Landström animates a country house in Strömstad with stacked and clashing roof angles and graphic decking and siding, uniting it all with a gray stain that matches the color of the corrugated metal roof.

OVERLEAF The decorative shingle siding (LEFT) of an eighteenth-century manor house (RIGHT) picks up on the curves and points of its terra-cotta-tiled mansard roof. For the sake of symmetry and rhythm, the windows that line up with the twin chimneys are blanks.

FLOURISHES IN
FORM AND COLOR

The windows of traditional wooden Scandinavian houses grew larger over time, but it is the entry upon which particular care was lavished. Drawing attention to the entrance can be as elaborate as fabricating a noteworthy front door, framing it in architectural detailing, or installing a porch that elevates arrivals and departures to the level of ceremony. Or it can be as simple as painting a door a bright color. Otherwise natural wood buildings adopt a jaunty air when their architectural details are highlighted with vivid hues.

The earliest doorways were natural wood embellished with carving (BOTTOM ROW CENTER). Later entries were flush with the façade and fitted out with expertly crafted doors, topped perhaps by a simple pediment (TOP ROW CENTER, BOTTOM ROW LEFT). The early-eighteenth-century passion for the Baroque generated fancy doorways appended to simple farmhouses (BOTTOM ROW RIGHT). Before a preference for front porches (TOP ROW RIGHT) gained ground in the nineteenth century, main entries were highlighted by decorative painted panels above and to the sides of the doorway (TOP ROW LEFT, MIDDLE ROW CENTER). By the late nineteenth century carpenters were demonstrating their prowess in wide-ranging styles—swags and other neo-Baroque flourishes framing windows (MIDDLE ROW LEFT) and brackets and detailing in neo-Viking Dragon style (MIDDLE ROW RIGHT).

OVERLEAF Falun red dominates the Swedish countryside. The linseed oil–based paint provides an effective, long-term seal against harsh weather and has a matte finish of surprising depth and luminosity, thanks to coarse crystals in the paint. Nothing is as striking as a red house hunkered down in a white wonderland.

FANCIFUL AND FANCY FREE

In the second half of the nineteenth century three factors came together to produce the most romantic and decorative architecture ever seen in Scandinavia: a growing desire for light and bright summer porches and pavilions, an increasing interest in exotic cultures, and advances in woodworking machinery that facilitated elaborate gingerbread trim.

TOP RIGHT AND OPPOSITE Known as the "Little Alhambra," Norwegian violinist Ole Bull's late-nineteenth-century summer house on the island of Lysøen presents the ultimate in skilled woodcraft and a lacy composite of styles (Venetian, Islamic, and Russian).

ABOVE LEFT AND RIGHT Natural wood benches and tables furnish an unpainted Finnish porch, reminiscent of a Russian dacha.

RIGHT A white porch dressed up in blue wicker is the model of a fresh summer veranda.

ROOTS AND SHOOTS

Norway's earliest farms were composed of unpainted timber buildings assembled around a courtyard and protected by a fence and gate. The main dwelling took up a central position; it was surrounded by separate structures, each with a distinct function: a stable, sheds for livestock and fodder, a forge, a sauna for drying meat and flax, a threshing house, and most important of all, a storehouse for grain and other valuables. The latter was rivaled only by the main dwelling in architectural stature and was always elevated on heavy timbers that were placed on stone footings to discourage infestations and rising damp. Fabricated originally of interlocking rough timbers, later of planed boards that provided better protection, the buildings featured peaked roofs topped with birch bark and then a layer of turf. Trimming the sod roofs was a biannual undertaking.

TOP Painted trim distinguishes the main dwelling at the center of this historic timber farm, which recognized the environmental advantages of sod roofs centuries ago.

BOTTOM LEFT Carved corner posts and stone footings and steps attest to the importance of a pair of storehouses in Norway.

BOTTOM RIGHT The planted roof of a contemporary Finnish cabin has grown so wild it fairly disappears into the landscape.

BRIDGING NATURE
AND THE PAST

Scandinavian country houses tend to come in two types: old and charming or new and modern. A house in Tofta, Sweden, demonstrates that the two are not mutually exclusive. By appending a light-as-air pavilion (OPPOSITE) to a traditional red farmhouse (BELOW), architects Gert and Karin Wingårdh provide the residents with a more direct connection to their waterfront land. A new glass-fronted bay framed in red (LEFT) marries old and new.

EMBRACING THE ELEMENTS

Waterfront sites, especially those subject to salt spray and steady wind, present particular architectural demands. The houses on these pages offer a primer in sheltering techniques.

OPPOSITE A framework of staggered panels of wood stained black creates a graphically powerful screen that functions as a windbreak.

ABOVE A vacation house, its jagged roofline in contrast to stone worn smooth over time, reduces its exposure by hunkering down atop a rocky outcropping.

BELOW LEFT Rooms are set on the diagonal along an elevated platform, creating a series of protected outdoor spaces.

BELOW RIGHT Exposed rafters reduce the impact of the wind as well as the exposure of huge windows to the sun.

TREADING LIGHTLY

In building new country houses Scandinavians go to great lengths to be at one with nature. Rather than imposing their designs on the land, they work with the surroundings, taking advantage of natural shelter by selecting sites just on the edge of a forest or nestled in the depression of a rock ledge. To disturb the land as little as possible, houses are sited, even designed, around existing trees and their roots, and often elevated on platforms. Dwellings with exposed wood frames reference the forest. Huge expanses of glass foster a sense of living among the trees and turn houses into lanterns at night.

TOP A house in Sweden hovers just above the forest floor, its deck wrapping around a pine tree that becomes a canopy for the outdoor eating area.

BOTTOM A "folded" wall of glass along one side of a low-slung house reflects and extends its woody setting.

OPPOSITE Amphitheatre-like wooden steps provide a comfortable place to study nature as well as a bridge between a house elevated on pilings and the forest around it.

OVERLEAF Wrapped in a net vinyl cloth photoprinted with images of the surrounding juniper forest, a house by architects Ulla Alberts and Hans Murman plays hide-and-seek in the landscape.

HOUSE OF SEA AND SKY

Nothing magnifies light like water. Scandinavians are drawn to the shore as much for its brightness as its recreational offerings. Happily, the abundance of coastline and, especially in Finland, lakes, brings the dream of a house by the water a giant step closer to realization.

Swedish architect Gert Wingårdh took full advantage of a sloping waterside site dominated by granite outcroppings to produce a dramatic design for a house near Gothenburg.

LEFT The approach offers no clue as to what lies on the opposite side. Uplights set in concrete guide visitors between hulking shoulders of granite to the front door of a small bunker-like structure.

ABOVE Only once inside are visitors exposed to a broad western vista of shoreline captured through a double-height hall and two glass-enclosed wings.

OPPOSITE A pool projecting to the edge of the water clouds the distinction between sea and sky.

ENTRANCES
AND STAIRCASES

To step into a Scandinavian house is to experience Nordic decoration and hospitality in a nutshell. As Scandinavians tend to invite only family and the closest of friends to their houses, it follows that the entrance hall itself is intimate and informal. In the most modest farmhouses, foyers are essentially vestibules that serve as a buffer to the outside, typically small in scale with low ceilings, often of wood, to retain heat. Stairways tuck efficiently into corners, following function more than form. The narrow staircases themselves are stripped to the essentials: bare wood treads and risers, plain balusters, and simple newel posts.

In similar fashion, decorating takes a pragmatic, if still stylish, direction: everything one needs and little else. There may be a small flat-weave rug to prevent slips on a wet surface, a chair for sitting to remove one's boots or to hold a package, and a table just large enough for a lamp, a dish to catch pocket change, and an inviting arrangement of wildflowers or pine boughs. Inevitably, there will be accommodation for candles, either in sconces or candlesticks. Case clocks and portraits act as hall sentries, populating the foyer even when it's empty. Pattern appears in floors and walls painted to mimic tile or stone, as well as in seat-cushion fabrics and area rugs.

In manor houses, the entry is less a modest room than a central hall, sometimes rising two stories, that anchors and reveals a more formal architectural plan, usually symmetrical rooms or wings flanking the hall. In keeping with the grander scale, materials are more substantial: plaster walls, graceful broad stairways in stone, and elegant wrought-iron railings.

A front door carved in the Neoclassical style opens into an entry hall populated with hallmarks of Swedish decorating: a classical plaster medallion hung on a spatter-painted rough timber wall and red country chairs lined up on a floor painted to mimic geometric tile.

A WARM WELCOME

Whether the palette is coolly Gustavian or a bolder hue like a traditional red, Scandinavian entry foyers always project a hospitable familial atmosphere. The key to shaping an inviting space: furnishing it like a real room instead of a transit area.

BELOW An area rug and side chair in subtle tones complement woodwork appreciated for its worn patina.

RIGHT A black-painted Rococo side chair and an Empire table with tripod dolphin base, as well as numerous glints of gold, elevate a front hall from modest entry to elegant foyer.

OVERLEAF, LEFT Against rough wood walls painted pale gray and furniture only a touch deeper, a plaster medallion with a faux-bronze finish contributes an outsize seal of refinement.

OVERLEAF, RIGHT Its gilded frame a striking contrast to natural stone walls, a portrait of one of Henry VIII's wives lends gravitas to a contemporary foyer.

A COOL RECEPTION

Architecture alone ennobles grand entry halls, but elegantly proportioned rooms rendered in fine materials still benefit from a bit of decorating. Portraits and busts are especially effective at bringing life to austere spaces, as is a touch of gold.

TOP, BOTTOM, AND OPPOSITE Gilded frames and classical busts, a pair of cast-iron pugs, and fanciful ironwork offset the austerity of stone stairways in two entry halls.

OVERLEAF, LEFT AND RIGHT The entrance hall of Svartsjö, a hunting lodge outside Stockholm built for King Fredrik I, is an elegant example of Nordic formality and restraint, especially as practiced by architect Carl Hårleman. Heavily influenced by a 1728 French pattern book on architecture, Hårleman composed an oval entry hall with symmetrical niches for statues leading to a two-story octagonal salon. The original stone floor was replaced in the 1770s by a wooden one; its radiating sections accentuate the plan of the room. Stripped to its essence, the suite of rooms can be all the better appreciated for its masterful handling of proportion, scale, and classical detailing.

BOLD MOVES

Relatively modest players in traditional houses, stairways take center stage in contemporary dwellings, becoming pivotal sculptural elements. They provide a platform that exposes and celebrates movement.

RIGHT A stair in a straight run ties together open spaces of a modern Swedish house, serving as an orienting spine. A long skylight above it accentuates its linearity, while a curved wall on the upper landing softens it.

OPPOSITE In a modern apartment in Stockholm, a spiral stair leading to a loft under the eaves makes a dramatic statement. Both graceful and muscular, its curves relieve the otherwise hard edges of the spare interior. The structure of a paper globe light echoes the spiral, if in a far more delicate fashion.

LIVING ROOMS

If there is one overwhelming characteristic of Scandinavian interiors, it is a calm restraint. Rooms reflect less a sense of holding back than a putting into place of what is necessary and little more, a modesty born of a rural populace accustomed to making things from materials at hand. An emphasis on the minimum leads to a circumspect approach to decorating. The end result: a greater appreciation of craft and a more refined eye.

Such a minimal approach starts with the furniture plan. Unlike the rambling houses of equatorial climes, Scandinavian houses contract against the cold, concentrating various activities in a central living area more easily heated by one source. The Nordic living room has always been an exemplar of using space wisely. Built-in furniture satisfies a need for warmth, efficiency, and economy, clearing the floor for easy maintenance and ready adjustment of free-standing furniture. For the highly phototropic Scandinavians, that means a seasonal shift. In winter, tables and chairs move closer to the glowing hearth; in summer, they migrate to the window or straight out into the garden.

Amplifying light is always the goal. Clutter obstructs space; objects are select—beautiful and functional but never superfluous. A porcelain bowl offers fruit; a hand-blown vase, wildflowers; a brass candlestick, the light of a candle, but even devoid of content they contribute—their lustrous finishes propel light around the room. Consoles laden with framed family photos or collections of bibelots are as rare as layered window treatments or skirted tables. Amid fewer competitors, furnishings' features—the graceful cabriole leg of a table, the organic form of a modern chair, the handsome profile of a classical bust—shine more brightly. Linked to the elements by walls painted shades of light and air, the Scandinavian living room is a thoughtfully edited, lovingly crafted nest of harmony and grace.

Brilliant notes of color—an orange Mora clock, a striking contemporary painting, a bright kilim, and a fauteuil upholstered in a bold plaid—paint an elegant eighteenth-century Danish apartment as a modern player.

THE GUSTAVIAN LOOK

Rooms in the Gustavian style are quiet yet strong, elegant yet casual in a soft manner that doesn't rely on the bloated furnishings of a more Anglo-American shabby chic style. The appeal of Gustavian style is widespread and obvious, as popular now as when it debuted in the eighteenth century, but its building blocks are the embodiment of subtlety. First, a palette of pale colors—blues, straw yellow, buff pink, working off a foundation of pearl gray—complemented by unvarnished wood floors and lime-washed ceilings. Second, painted furniture with a matte, even slightly worn finish. Third, furnishings that display a simple but graceful form and minimal detailing like fluting and beading. Fourth, a symmetrical furniture arrangement that lends calm to a room, and finally, a measured dose of pattern, in fabrics and accessories, that contributes a light-hearted but not busy note.

OPPOSITE Though many of the elements in this eighteenth-century Swedish living room display age and wear, the overall effect is fresh and inviting. A delicate floral fabric for the sofa's squabs, along with pieces of blue and white porcelain, brightens the otherwise muted tone.

TOP, CENTER, AND BOTTOM Swedes distilled Rococo style to a lean elegance as captured in a demilune table, a desk and chair, and a tea table.

THE WOOD STOVE

Radiant floors and other technological advances in heating have enabled contemporary architects to plunk glass houses down in the most hostile northern latitudes. Still, rare is the Scandinavian who opts out of installing some sort of wood-burning stove in his home. The acts of chopping wood, building a fire, and stoking it to burn through the night maintain a humbling connection to nature and the labors of the past, in addition to addressing environmental responsibility. The rewards—the glow of a hearth and the intoxicating scent of wood smoke—are immediate, evocative, and all-embracing. Whether traditional or modern, of tiles or cast iron, wood stoves, more than any other object in the home, engage all the senses.

Carl Johan Cronstedt's invention of the tiled stove (*kakelugn*) in the mid-eighteenth century was the radical innovation of its day. In place of an open hearth, far more efficient vertical stoves of heat-retaining bricks covered in glazed tiles made the expansion (in both size and number) of rooms possible, forever revolutionizing the floor plan of Swedish houses.

RIGHT AND OPPOSITE, TOP ROW LEFT AND RIGHT, MIDDLE ROW RIGHT, AND BOTTOM ROW RIGHT
The Marieberg factory produced much of the faience tile for early Swedish stoves.

OPPOSITE, TOP ROW CENTER AND MIDDLE ROW LEFT
Highly decorated cast-iron stoves were always more common in Norway.

OPPOSITE, MIDDLE ROW CENTER A faux-painted cupboard masquerading as a fireplace maintains perfect symmetry in a Gustavian dining room.

OPPOSITE, BOTTOM ROW LEFT AND CENTER Contemporary stoves tend to be monolithic, though they vary in size and material.

A PERFECT BALANCE

The French are formal, the Swedes are orderly. Though the former heavily influenced the latter in the eighteenth century, driven by King Carl Gustav III's enduring impressions of his stay at Versailles, the Swedish version of royal decorating has always toned down the gilt and glamour and played up a refined serenity. Symmetry alone has a powerful calming effect, a decorating approach that's long been practiced in Sweden. Two objects flanking a central point of focus is enough to establish symmetry. The elements needn't even be a matching pair, just similar enough to create a satisfying ying/yang balance.

The Gustavian period favored arranging furniture around the perimeter of the room, symmetrically flanking a focal point such as the window in Carl Linnaeus's study (ABOVE) or dining room (OPPOSITE, TOP), or a console and pier mirror (OPPOSITE, BOTTOM).

OVERLEAF Trompe l'oeil columns, statues, and overdoors reinforce the symmetry of the architecture in the hall at Åkerö, as does a bolder marble floor.

LIGHT THE WAY

The contemporary house in Scandinavia simply can't have enough daylight. Thermal windows and radiant floors allow for whole walls of glass, assigning nature the role of primary interior decorator. Little can compete with walls given over to glorious panoramas of sea and sky, forest and fields. (First rule of building: choose your site wisely.) White walls enable natural light to set the tone, turning open spaces, like mood rings, into settings of ever-shifting character. Skylights and triple-glazed windows ensure that modern interiors in older dwellings can be just as bright. Obscuring the view in any way is anathema, so window coverings are rare. (Again, choose your site wisely.) Essential, though, is a fireplace or wood stove to complete the elements—earth, water, air, fire.

TOP Blue bands of sea and sky create a natural dado for the glazed gable wall of a spacious open-plan kitchen/dining/living room in Denmark.

BOTTOM, LEFT TO RIGHT A freestanding fireplace is the only divider in a living/dining space that soars to the roof peak. Two enormous and unadorned plate-glass windows ensure that the spare living area of a Swedish house is blindingly bright even on a cloudy day. In a loft at the top of a building in Stockholm, a combination of windows, dormers, and skylights draws the eye up and out.

DANISH RULE

Danish Modern so blanketed the 1950s and 1960s that it's hard now to realize how radical its first examples were. Finn Juhl, a trained architect but self-taught furniture designer, broke with tradition in emphasizing form over function and exploring all the properties of a then-exotic wood, teak. The graceful lines and natural shapes of his award-winning furniture drew international attention to Danish design, launching a tsunami of furnishings, particularly in teak, from now-classic masterworks by Juhl and other Danish designers to an undertow of cheap imitations. So prized are the organic forms (and so widespread was the production, making the furniture relatively affordable) that few Danish interiors dating from the mid-century on are without a piece or two by notable native designers.

CLOCKWISE FROM UPPER LEFT Juhl kept it light and bright in his own living room, upholstering his Poeten sofa and leather Chieftain chair in pale shades, then adding a strong rug and portrait. A streamlined table fairly disappears into a wall of books in Hanne and Poul Kjaerholm's house in Denmark, while a fluttering Poul Henningsen light fixture hovers before it. The strict lines of a wall-hung cabinet are softened by warm wood grain and a trio of ceramic vessels. Upholstered in vivid red, Hans Wegner's Ox chair makes a white living area come alive; a black floor sets off a set of his Wishbone chairs in white. Chairs by Finnish designer Antti Nurmesniemi are as boldly graphic as the ceiling's truss system. Tubular steel furniture echoes the form of an embellished column and free-standing fireplace. Mid-century Danish furniture is as at home in a nineteenth-century interior as in a modern one. A teak tabouret by Finn Juhl opens to reveal a rainbow of colorful drawers.

THE TEST OF TIME

Like oak leaves, the lobes of Danish furniture are infinitely variable yet instantly indicative of a genus. Pleasing to the eye, the organic shapes are every bit as accommodating to the body. Early experiments with teak expanded to include other woods as well as steel, a material favored by Danish designer Poul Kjaerholm for its elegance and light-catching quality. So timeless are the designs that, when paired with contemporary art and objects, the furniture too looks absolutely of the moment.

OPPOSITE, TOP In a Danish living room, the only truly contemporary object is artwork. Arne Jacobsen's upholstered pieces, flanked by two of his floor lamps, are completely at home atop a Blackboard rug designed by Eileen Gray in the 1920s.

OPPOSITE, BOTTOM, LEFT TO RIGHT Natural materials like caning and sisal matting temper the cool steel of Kjaerholm's Hammock chair. A 1953 chair by Finn Juhl is composed of beech and rosewood. Arne Jacobsen's Egg chair and ottoman is as much nest as egg.

THIS PAGE, TOP A painted plywood chair by Poul Kjaerholm is so strong in form, it needs to stand alone.

THIS PAGE, BOTTOM With his PK9 chairs and PK54 table, Poul Kjaerholm played with geometry and a mix of materials.

DANISH MODERN CHAIRS

Turn over almost any piece of fine mid-century modern Danish furniture and you will find credited not only the name of the designer but also the actual maker. Denmark's heritage of cabinetmaking, along with its emphasis on training architects in all aspects of design, is unmatched in Scandinavia, nurtured by the Royal Danish Academy of Fine Arts since its establishment in 1754. Nearly every iconic chair classified as Scandinavian Modern is actually Danish, the product of a collaboration between designers who were usually architects and master cabinetmakers who were as exalted as the designers. Architect and self-taught furniture designer Finn Juhl teamed with Niels Vodder to create the 45-Chair (TOP ROW CENTER), a triumph of woodworking as well as organic form. Hans Wegner's success as the most prolific Danish furniture designer (more than 500 designs) was no doubt an outgrowth of his initial training as a cabinetmaker and his longtime collaboration with maker Johannes Hansen. Together they produced the remarkable Peacock Chair (MIDDLE ROW LEFT), a 1947 design still in production, and the Shell Chair, 1948 (MIDDLE ROW RIGHT), a prime example of Wegner's penchant for mixing woods, here solid beech and bent teak.

Wegner's Papa Bear chair, 1954 (TOP ROW RIGHT), like Arne Jacobsen's Egg Chair, 1960 (TOP ROW LEFT), designed for the Royal Hotel in Copenhagen, celebrate the assuring embrace of nature—Wegner's with a warm and wooly bear hug and Jacobsen's with a leather cocoon of natural geometry that grows deeper and richer with time. More abstract in its embrace is Verner Panton's Heart Cone Chair, 1959 (BOTTOM ROW RIGHT), a take on the traditional wing chair that, like most of Panton's work, is playful, colorful, and experimental without sacrificing comfort. Even his Panton Chair, 1960 (MIDDLE ROW CENTER), a radical swoop of bright plastic, was a fun sit as well as eminently practical—the molded forms easily stacked. While most Danish designers were seduced by the properties and possibilities of wood, Poul Kjaerholm, together with maker E. Kold Christensen, produced clean designs such as lounge chairs PK22, 1955, and PK20, 1967 (BOTTOM ROW LEFT AND CENTER), that laud the strength, lightness, and elegance of steel.

ABOVE IT ALL

Considered the fifth wall, ceilings in Scandinavia receive as much attention as the other planes of the room, sometimes more. The treatment may be as simple as leaving wide boards—installed parallel with the floorboards—to darken naturally, creating a cozy cabin effect. Whitewashing boards and beams lifts the eye and lightens a room. A strong color overhead, especially when it's united with a wall color, can completely reconfigure a room and one's experience of it. Designs for mid-twentieth-century houses tinkered with reversing the previous roles of a room's surfaces, leaving walls white and creating finely crafted wood ceilings.

ABOVE In a Swedish farmhouse a white ceiling ameliorates the squat dimensions of the room and balances a boldly checked floor.

OPPOSITE, TOP Trails of darkened nail holes traveling across pine boards create a subtle plaid pattern on the drawing room ceiling at Linnaeus's Hammarby.

OPPOSITE, BOTTOM LEFT Sunlight penetrating a frieze of curved metal throws searchlight beams across the ceiling of Alvar Aalto's Villa Mairea in Finland.

OPPOSITE, BOTTOM RIGHT Foil to a rich red interior wall color, a brilliant green seen through the doorway is a tipoff that one is about to step outside into a breezeway with views of a lawn.

A LITTLE BIT
SOFTER NOW

A color can be definitive without being bold. A rosy
terra-cotta such as the wall color of this entry hall
(OPPOSITE) is as welcoming as a strong red and a better complement to warm gray trim. Grayed blues
tilting toward a sky hue in a Finnish salon (RIGHT)
and periwinkle in a Swedish manor house (BELOW)
project a fresh elegance without being cold.

COLORS OF OLD

Gray and blue and all the soft shades they make together are the colors most often associated with Swedish, and in particular Gustavian, style. In an environment blanketed with snow for many months, gray is easier on the eyes than white, especially on blinding sunny days, yet it still carries the light. Moreover, it's practical, brightening interiors without showing the dirt. But nothing enhances a hue as well as its complement on the color wheel, which may explain why Swedes have long been as drawn to warm buffs and yellows as cooler colors. A reflection of their unpretentious and thrifty instincts, a shade of yellow ochre paint often stood in for gilding, capturing the richness of gold while eschewing its extravagance.

Two-tone walls in warm, natural hues, along with an untreated wood floor and ceiling set off furnishings painted a steely gray. A thin gray line sharply defines the top of the dado (BELOW). Painting the woodwork framing deep window sills colors the light entering the room (OPPOSITE, TOP AND RIGHT). Blue walls veering toward lavender are one of many elegant details chosen for this room in Regnaholm (OPPOSITE, BOTTOM).

GO BOLD

Though more often seen in modern interiors, intense colors are that much more daring in rooms of older houses furnished with antiques, if only because they're less expected. In Norway, though, the use of strong color has a long tradition. Like a stunning and exceptionally warm winter coat, an interior dressed in hues as rich as scarlet or cobalt blue is simultaneously stimulating and comforting.

In a Norwegian farmhouse sitting room (LEFT) and a suite of salons in a manor house (BELOW), deep wall colors embrace dark wood furniture. Touches of brass and gold and patterned rugs and fabrics provide sparks of light.

GOOD FOLK

Being confined indoors through long, dark winters drives some to drink, others to industry. Scandinavians made the most of imposed hibernation by developing their folk-painting styles— *rosemaling* in Norway, *kurbits* in Sweden—spread throughout the countryside by itinerant painters. The charm of hand-painted scenes and figures is undeniable. A skilled but loose hand with the brush and a free approach to color can transform an ordinary room into a beguiling space, a piece of furniture into an heirloom. As enlivening as wallpaper, though more informal, a profusion of color and pattern on walls and ceilings can counterbalance a quiet room or, alternatively, liberate a room to pile on even more layers of texture. Sometimes, even in Scandinavia, more is more.

TOP A lineup of winsome, near life-size figures, like those embellishing one wall of a historic Norwegian timber farmhouse, often commemorates a wedding or other important family event.

BOTTOM Birds in flight and tendrils of flowers across a field of blue offset the somber portrait of a woman.

OPPOSITE Sailors and a ship caught amid floral flourishes reference the coastal location of a barn in Norway.

SLEIGHT OF HAND

Scandinavia is a treasure trove of trompe l'oeil masterpieces, each a demonstration that making do need not mean doing with less. A skilled painter can turn plain floors into fancy parquet, humble rooms into noble salons. Classical motifs took hold in Scandinavia, as in the rest of Europe, in the late eighteenth century. But in the absence of local marble or a generous budget, builders employed craftsmen to mimic architectural elements and carved and cast decorations using only paint, applied to wood, canvas, and paper.

LEFT The only features of a Swedish-influenced Finnish salon that are actually three-dimensional are the columns flanking the fireplace, the doors, and the corbels of the cornice.

RIGHT Common tools (a bellows, a bucket) grow in stature when rendered, in paint on paper, as a classical festoon for an upper hall in Svartå manor house in southern Finland.

BELOW A cast-iron stove fairly disappears into a grisaille wall of fanciful foliage over a drapery dado.

CHINA SEAS

Nothing wakes an interior from a domestic stupor more effectively than a dose of the wholly unfamiliar. Like a bold modern painting hung against boiserie or a Jacobean table in a minimalist dining room, it's contrast that counts. In Sweden and Denmark, the foreign agent spicing palaces and manor houses for nearly a century was the Far East. From 1731 to 1813 the ships of the Swedish East India Company hauled nearly fifty million pieces of porcelain from Canton to satisfy a widening taste for chinoiserie. Everyday households had a Chinese export bowl or two; the elite commissioned whole rooms painted in fanciful Chinese scenes and motifs.

LEFT AND BELOW Imaginary landscapes populated by Chinese figures inject rooms at Thureholm with a captivating exoticism. So rich and deep is their palette that these wall paintings read initially as Baroque.

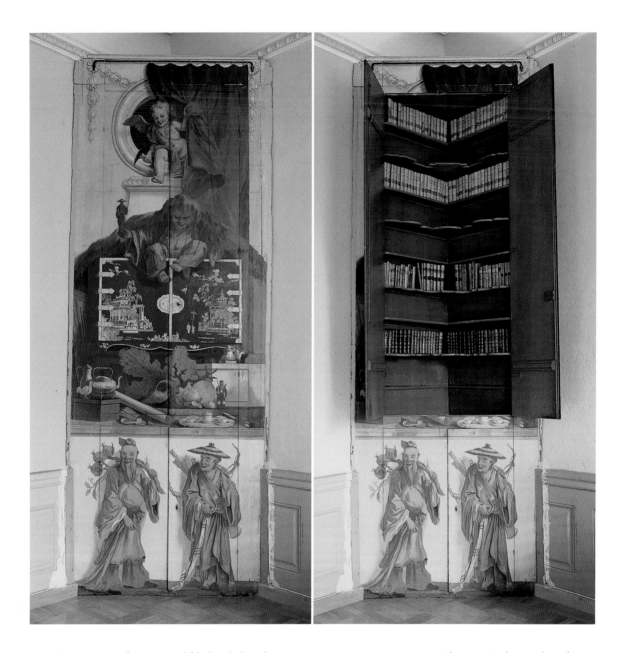

Discovering a fantasy world behind closed doors is like lifting the lid of a jewel box. Tucked away in Swedish manor houses are interpretations of a far-off land rendered in a startling range of reds, blacks, and golds.

ABOVE LEFT AND RIGHT Like an artist's sampler of techniques, a single corner cupboard at Åkerö displays experiments with imagery, scale, and materials.

OPPOSITE Black lacquer and gilding applied to moldings and Rococo furnishings are the sophisticated mate to exotic wallpaper, turning a room at Thureholm into a chic treasure chest.

PAPER AND PAINT

Though much inspired by other lands, especially France, Italy, and China, Scandinavians have always adapted decorating styles to their own sparer aesthetic and thrifty impulses. Nordic interiors are an encyclopedic demonstration of all that can be done with a material as affordable and available as paint. From applying it directly to wood, Scandinavian artisans progressed to painting on canvas, a modest means of imitating architectural paneling, tapestries and hangings, intricate carving, and fanciful motifs. Linen panels stretched on the wall above a dado featured panoramic scenes favored in Rococo interiors and classical and horticultural detail characteristic of the Gustavian period. Factory-printed wallpaper accelerated a taste for subtle overall pattern that remains in favor, but sometimes something as simple as highlighting the lines of a room with a delicate border is all that it takes to transform an ordinary space into an extraordinary one.

OPPOSITE In the Chinese cabinet at Regnaholm, a filigree of Asian motifs painted in oil on linen reflects the Rococo taste for the exotic.

TOP A wallpaper of white wisps on pale blue sets a bright Jugendstil sunroom in Finland adrift on a cloud.

BOTTOM Trim and furniture painted white highlight the white blossoms scattered across antique French wallpapers in soft blue and spring green.

OVERLEAF, LEFT AND RIGHT From a bucolic waterfront setting to an interpretation of an English hunt, richly rendered scenes can transport rooms to other places and times.

GOLD STANDARD

Against a palette predominantly of pale grays and blues, gold glows even more warmly. An interior accented with touches of gilt, as well as mirrors and crystals, sends candlelight off on a lighthearted dance like a butterfly flitting from blossom to blossom.

Except for the interiors of palaces and select manor houses like Norway's Bogstad (RIGHT), where gilded frames line the ballroom, gilding was used sparingly, most often to pick out a bit of molding or for the frames of mirrored sconces (LEFT) and paintings and photographs (BELOW).

BACK FROM
THE HUNT

Decorating a hunting lodge in Scandinavia is a straightforward proposition: use what you've got. When assembled in rhythmic formation on a solid-colored wall, guns and swords can be appreciated for what they often are, works of art in their own right. The shift in focus allows their elegant forms and decorative qualities to override their primary function. Similarly, the spoils of the hunt assume an anthropological aspect when put on display, layering a nature study with references to rituals and history. Like tree branches or human hands, elk antlers demonstrate a variation on a theme that is both powerful and absorbing.

OPPOSITE A ship hung from a beam adds a note of levity to a hall decorated in militaristic fashion.

TOP Trophies of hunts over the decades, elk antlers and skulls contribute a wild dimension to the stair hall of a family hunting lodge in Norway.

BOTTOM Antique rifles appear at the ready in a room of Norwegian manor house Skinnarbol, watched over by mounted elk heads.

DINING ROOMS

Dining rooms in Scandinavia tend to swing between two opposite yet equally enchanting worlds: one dark and a bit mysterious, lit by a steady fire and many candles; the other, brilliant and airy, awash in the soft light of endless midsummer evenings. The former evokes the times of the Vikings, when houses were, first and foremost, shelters from the weather, their windows small, their interiors dim. Dining then meant sitting on simple stools pulled up to the hearth. Rustic trestle and sawbuck tables still furnish the dining rooms of farmhouses and country cabins, as do unpainted hand-carved chairs and practical banquettes, the descendants of built-in benches that once served triple-duty (seating, storage, sleeping).

In Norway especially, the nineteenth century experienced a renewed pride in Viking motifs and craft, resulting in manor-house dining halls heavily decorated in the Dragon style, complete with fanciful beams and brackets, deeply carved benches, tables, and chairs, tapestries capturing Norwegian mythology, and elaborate brass chandeliers and sconces. The same period in Sweden produced dining rooms equally dark and rich, though the taste was more for Renaissance Revival furnishings and walls skillfully painted to mimic marble or French tapestries.

Though Scandinavians use candles and firelight to great effect in lifting their spirits during long winters, it is the long days of summer they cherish most. And it is the dining rooms that capture and craft light that we most associate with the Nordic countries, especially Sweden. Gustavian rooms celebrated a delicate pale palette in woodwork and furnishings and a pleasing symmetry in furniture arrangement. Pairs of servers remained against the walls, as did pairs of demilune tables until they were brought together to form full circles for dining. Similarly, gateleg tables that, folded down and placed against a wall, took up precious little space, opened up and joined to form long banquet tables. With the midnight sun streaming in through generous windows all evening, only a smattering of mirrors and crystals were required for a touch of glittering amplification.

A dogtrot-style breezeway in Gert and Karin Wingårdh's contemporary addition to a traditional Swedish farmhouse brings dining closer to nature, with no need to run for cover. The painted walls and ceiling pick up the color of grass outside, framing the view in bright green.

RICH TRADITION

Three Norwegian dining rooms draw on folk tradition for a suite of furniture carved in the nationalist Dragon style (RIGHT), a saturated color palette (especially deep blues, gold and reds), and motifs ranging from homespun garlands (BELOW) to more stylized ornamentation (OPPOSITE).

ELEGANT ENTERTAINING

The main salon at Regnaholm, a 1760s manor house now owned by a former curator at the National Museum of Antiquities in Stockholm, is the perfect expression of the refinement, symmetry, and lightness of early Gustavian style that evolved from Swedish Rococo. Tall, unadorned windows admit copious light that pale painted walls, a white ceiling, and scrubbed, untreated wood floors further transmit. In the evening, mirror-backed gilded candle sconces and a central chandelier laden with refracting crystals cast a sparkly glow. Furniture was traditionally arranged symmetrically around the perimeter of the room, thereby freeing space for receptions and dancing. For dinner parties, the gateleg tables and suites of chairs moved to center stage. Presiding over it all is a magnificent bust of Karl Johan XIV mounted on a truncated fluted column.

OVERLEAF Painted "tapestry" walls and faux marbling along with heavy baronial furnishings, whether ebonized and gilded (LEFT) or left in a natural state (RIGHT), reflect a Renaissance Revival fashionable in the late nineteenth century.

NORTHERN LIGHTS

Suites of furniture painted white and light gray, set against pale walls, capture the feel of a midsummer night year round. Painting furniture a light color was historically a way to unite disparate styles and mask the common or mismatched woods of which the pieces were made, as pine and spruce were far more available than the mahogany popular on the Continent. The eighteenth-century taste in dining chairs was for English models made by the reigning craftsmen—Chippendale, Hepplewhite, and Shera-ton—though the Swedish versions were inevitably sparer in decoration and more countrified because of their paint finish. Medallion chairs in a farmhouse dining room (THIS PAGE, TOP) and a set of chairs with wheat sheaf carved splats (OPPOSITE, BOTTOM LEFT) are hallmarks of early Gustavian style. Chippendale-style chairs (THIS PAGE, CENTER) and shield-back chairs in the manner of Hepplewhite (OPPOSITE, TOP) furnish more formal dining rooms. Two youth chairs join simple folding chairs in a rustic modern kitchen (THIS PAGE, BOTTOM). A tall built-in sideboard and stylized Chippendale chairs, all painted white, represent the late-nineteenth-century taste for bright and light interiors for summer houses in the Swedish archipelago (OPPOSITE, BOTTOM RIGHT).

SETTING THE STAGE

Stark contrast—light against dark, dark against light—works to striking effect in two dining rooms, one grand, one more modest.

LEFT Around a crossbuck table, simple chairs painted white are as rhythmic as ships lined up for the famous 1801 Battle of Copenhagen, captured in a wall mural that has the effect of a giant picture window. The aquatic hues of the mural, an oil-on-canvas tapestry imitation popular in the eighteenth century, extend the blues of the dining room in the 1797 Brødretomten villa on the edge of Bergen.

BELOW In a more casual Swedish dining room, the crossbuck table is painted white, as is nearly everything but the dining chairs. The parade of Xs formed by the chairs' graphic backs offsets the streamlined banquette they sit opposite.

DESIGN ELEMENT
PAINTED FURNITURE

Painting furniture pale colors has always been a means of visually extending limited daylight, but it is never solely an aesthetic decision. For the ever frugal and pragmatic Scandinavian, who rarely disposes of furniture, redecorating means refreshing and replacing fabrics and repainting furniture to suit. The earliest painting was done to mask the fact that furniture was made of common pine or disparate woods.

Shadows highlighting the carving of a console (RIGHT) celebrate detailing every bit as lively as, and richer in dimension than, painted pattern. Soft whites and pale shades of gray, like that of the Gustavian settee (OPPOSITE, MIDDLE ROW CENTER AND BOTTOM ROW LEFT) along with open-back chairs in a variety of styles, have come to define a lightness characteristic of Swedish style.

MODERN MIX

Choice modern pieces—pendant lighting, art glass, contemporary artwork—bring traditional interiors into the twenty-first century. Light fixtures by Poul Henningsen, like his PH5 from 1958 (BELOW) are common in Danish homes, no matter what their style. Super-scaled shades, like the trio in a contemporary Swedish house (LEFT) are less expected. In an eighteenth-century Danish apartment, a variety of prints and drawings tempers the formality of the architecture (RIGHT).

NEW OLD WORLD

Lining a beautifully proportioned salon in a mid-
nineteenth-century Stockholm apartment with
elegant bookcases expands a dining room into a
library, turning a seldom-used space into an oft-
used one. By day, multiple sconces aid referencing
materials on the shelves; at night, the small pools
of light highlight the texture of varied spines,
adding interest and dimension. The use of warm
woods, soft wallpaper, and rich accent colors
(ruby curtains, sapphire seat cushions, emerald
lampshades) makes the space inviting at any hour.

CLEAN PLATE

Reducing all surfaces to simple planes sets a modern stage on which diners and food become the colorful main players. Sleek cabinetry and appliances enable kitchens in contemporary interiors to be both open and discreet. In such spare environments, dining tables assume sculptural importance, and natural light is as significant a component of the palette as any color.

ABOVE Like a lowered drawbridge, the deck of Juniper House on Gotland, by Ulla Alberts and Hans Murman, opens up the dining room, extending it into the surrounding forest.

RIGHT In a Stockholm apartment recently renovated by the notable Swedish architecture firm Claesson Koivisto Rune, the kitchen is a floor-to-ceiling armoire, its glossy counter an elegant server for the dining area. Large, framed photographs mimic the window openings opposite them while flush wall lights re-create the glow of eighteenth-century sconces between windows.

WOOD WONDERS

In interiors that range from elaborate to severely modern to rustic, Scandinavians display a mastery of natural woodcraft rivaled perhaps only by the Japanese. The woodwork of the music salon in nineteenth-century Norwegian violinist Ole Bull's summer home south of Bergen (LEFT) exceeds a pair of crystal chandeliers in fanciful detail. Reflecting a late-nineteenth-century taste for eclecticism and revival styles, the room stitches together braided Italian-style columns, Moorish arches, and Venetian windows. The stepped area of a modern Norwegian house (BELOW) is as finely executed as a precise dovetail. In a cabin belonging to Finnish textile designer Ritva Puotila and her family (RIGHT), twin pedestals carved from roots support the thick slab of a weighty table as rustic as the interior.

A MODEL DINING ROOM

As befits the father of modern biological classification, Carl Linnaeus, even his dining room at Hammarby is a progenitor. A calm order and restrained decor still define Swedish dining rooms. Here, a pair of tables with expandable tops, looking far more contemporary than their 250 years, emphasizes the symmetry established by two windows. Flanking them, three chairs, two portraits, and a case clock establish a rhythm that breaks the symmetry oh so subtly (the clock). A simple striped paper picks up the line of parallel floor- and ceiling boards, aiding the eye in sweeping the room.

SOFTENED GRANDEUR

Formality in Sweden always arrives sensitively and sensibly dressed down, as this airy suite of rooms in a house dating from about 1770 demonstrates. A bare wood floor and simple white linen slipcovers balance the glitter of crystal and gleam of silver and polished mahogany. Moldings and an antique sideboard painted varied shades of blue complement the hues of the magnificent yet lighthearted chinoiserie wall paintings original to the house.

SPLENDOR ON THE WALLS

Damsgård, an opulent landmark wood manor, was built from 1770 to 1780 as a grand summer house overlooking Bergen's harbor. Its remarkably well-preserved rooms capture Rococo style in Norway at its finest, particularly the penchant for decorating rooms with a variety of impressive wall treatments from scenes painted on canvas above faux stone dados to expensive wallpapers.

LEFT In an enfilade of four drawing rooms used for entertaining, the first two rooms display a neoclassical restraint.

BELOW The English wallpaper of the *Blåstuen* (blue salon), which follows, is unusual for its depth of color, boldness of scale, and a pattern that matches in exuberance the room's fine Baroque side chairs.

MORA CLOCKS

At its peak of production in the late eighteenth century, the town of Mora in the Swedish province of Dalarna, an area known for its strong craft traditions, turned out nearly a thousand tall case clocks a year. More precisely, the local farmers, who were both resourceful and skilled with a variety of tools and materials, crafted the clock works (brass mechanism, iron or soapstone weights, sheet-iron dial, brass hands) as a means of supplementing their incomes. The tall wooden cases were commissioned separately from carpenters both local and distant; the cases built in the north of Sweden were rather strict and lean, while those created elsewhere tended to have the full-bodied form heavily favored in the Rococo period. Mora clocks, the first affordable timekeeping devices for the average household, were often presented as wedding gifts and were the pride of rural farmsteads.

LEFT An eighteenth-century case clock in chalky blue with gilded accents exhibits the elegant curves of the classic Mora style.

OPPOSITE, TOP ROW, LEFT TO RIGHT Unusual early-nineteenth-century clock with fluted half-cylindrical body topped by a carved and gilded crown; "Blackcock" carved clock, ca. 1820, from Norrbotten in northeast Sweden; early (ca. 1800) Mora clock in original green and salmon paint; Mora clock, 1841, with naïve decoration.

OPPOSITE, BOTTOM ROW, LEFT TO RIGHT Early-nineteenth-century clock embellished with carved roses and leaves; Mora clock, 1809, with elaborate folkloric painting; gray-painted neoclassical clock, ca. 1810, with carving of lyre on plinth; clock, ca. 1760, topped by bridal crown of roses and foliage from Jämtland, Sweden.

LONG SUMMER NIGHTS

Scandinavians live for their summers, two short months of endless days and surprisingly temperate air, thanks to the North Atlantic Drift of the Gulf Stream. In this brief season, life is lived outdoors as much as possible. For dining *en plein air*, Scandinavians see no reason to sacrifice comfort and elegance; dining on a deck or porch encompasses every nicety of a proper meal indoors. And in the rare absence of a structured outdoor dining area, they simply create one, moving furniture to a field or patch of grass and crowning the setting with a chandelier strung up in a tree.

A picnic becomes an elegant repast with the addition of a fanciful chandelier to the humblest table and folding chairs (LEFT) or the transfer of fine crystal and a heavy tablecloth from their usual indoor setting to a less expected one beneath the trees (BELOW).

OVERLEAF A sheltered outdoor eating area like a porch (TOP LEFT AND BOTTOM RIGHT), a covered deck area (BOTTOM LEFT), or a courtyard (BOTTOM CENTER) is a priority for Scandinavians, who prize being close to nature. On a sunny day, though, any spot will do, especially one as colorful and enchanting as a field of poppies (TOP RIGHT).

KITCHENS

The overriding duty of Scandinavian kitchens is functional efficiency, yet one would be hard pressed to find examples that are cold or characterless. Whether historic or contemporary, urban or country, Nordic kitchens express the visual equivalent of bread baking in the oven. Their warm hominess, especially welcome in a colder clime, is fueled as much by personal objects and natural colors and materials as by a glowing fire or sun streaming in across countertops.

The kitchen, by virtue of its all-important hearth, has always been the heart of the house. An all-purpose work table was one of the first substantial pieces of furniture in Scandinavia not directly incorporated, like benches and beds, into the architecture of the house. The stone-topped table in the kitchen at Regnaholm (see pages 148–49) is a fine example. Though the long work table evolved in the eighteenth century into more portable versions, like the gateleg table for dining, furniture remained positioned against the walls, except during occasions such as dinner parties.

The painted, wood-framed daybed most commonly associated with the Gustavian period has its roots in the Swedish kitchen sofa, itself derived from built-in benches. Used as kitchen seating by day, the sofa (shown in its simplest form on page 84), was pulled out at night to take on the role of bed.

What lends character to Scandinavian kitchens even more than furniture is their tableware, one of the few things consistently put on display (see Plate Racks, pages 130–31). Among the most valuable and treasured objects in the house, plates of brass and pewter, faience from Sweden's own Marieberg and Rörstrand factories, and Chinese export porcelain were and remain like exquisite wallpaper for the kitchen, especially when mounted in racks and shelves that show off their faces. For an astonishing marriage of decorating and collecting nothing holds a candle to the porcelain kitchen at Thureholm, entirely faux-painted in the 1740s in a blue and white riff on the willow pattern (see page 9).

A taupe-colored sideboard with practical open shelves and integrated plate rack makes a fine display for shapely serveware in every shade of white and cream.

BRIDGING
TRADITION

An approach to kitchen renovation that blends the best of the old and the new produces a room that not only works hard but feels welcoming. In a mid-nineteenth-century apartment in Stockholm (LEFT AND OPPOSITE) the centrality of the kitchen to modern family life is recognized by awarding it the generous space of a traditional salon rather than relegating it to a service area. Though the elements of the new kitchen are kept to a contemporary minimum, they complement the scale of the room: oversize stove hood, tall cabinets, sizable worktable. Sleek cupboards keep clutter to a minimum, but where traditional open storage is needed most—to either side of the stove— it stakes its claim. The deep forest green of the cabinetry, along with the natural pine of the floor and table, tempers the industrial feel of the stainless-steel counter, stove, and hood. Lighting is discreet and purely functional in a room washed with daylight that's further extended by glossy surfaces. Contributing a lighthearted and distinctly Scandinavian effect are a wall dramatically "papered" with sprightly tiles applied in a random pattern and a printed curtain in similar colors that provides the requisite nod to nature: a cascade of leaves blowing by the window.

DESIGN ELEMENT
PLATE RACKS

Nearly every Nordic kitchen, from that in the simplest cabin to those of the grandest palaces and castles, features some form of open storage for tableware, with the plate rack reigning supreme first as an organizational aid and second as a decorative element. More than any other object, dishware embodies a combination of beauty and usefulness that suits the Scandinavian sensibility; it is one of the very few things that has long been not just acquired but collected and displayed.

Originally, given the ubiquity of wood tableware, metalware was most prized and proudly displayed. Sweden's legendary mine at Falun was turning out copper as early as the eleventh century and quickly grew into Europe's largest supplier—and Sweden's most important income producer. The expense of silver elevated pewter, its closest imitator, to most-valued status, at least until the end of the eighteenth century. Serious competition for best tableware arrived with the founding of the Swedish East India Company in 1731 and the subsequent steady influx of Chinese export porcelain (more than fifty million pieces in the period 1731–1813), generating a passion for blue and white china that has never waned. For the wealthy, displaying porcelain they had collected, in custom-made racks and even special porcelain rooms, became a rare demonstration of their riches.

In kitchens with a natural palette (RIGHT), putting colorful cookware on display gives the room an engaging focal point, as effective as hanging a brilliant painting in a serene living room.

OPEN KITCHEN

In the kitchens of modern Scandinavian houses, the cook's contact with other family members and guests is as essential as proximity to nature. A substantial counter that serves double duty as a workspace and serving area is often all that divides the kitchen from the living and dining areas in one large, open space. Behind the counter, a row of cabinets and appliances establishes a galley arrangement that is both neat and efficient.

Animating the typically monochromatic environment of the contemporary kitchens on these pages are the shifting hues and angles of daylight streaming in through huge skylights and windows.

CLOSE TO NATURE

Windows in contemporary houses are carefully planned to both draw in and frame the surrounding landscape, liberating kitchens from the darkest core of the house. No matter the size of the opening, the view to the outside means cooks benefit from the companionship of nature even when they're working solo.

OPPOSITE Giant glass doors slide apart to eliminate an entire wall of the kitchen in Casa Barone, a summer house near Stockholm by WRB (Widjedal, Racki, and Bergerhoff) Architects .

ABOVE A narrow band of windows lights the work surface of a kitchen in Norway and, together with the clerestory windows, the table flanked by benches, and even the counter-height hearth, emphasizes the horizontality of the overall design.

DANISH BLEND

In two Danish kitchens of similar size and volume though different centuries, the prep area is relegated to a side or corner while the table stakes out center stage. Furnishing the rooms with artwork, antiques, and iconic mid-century lighting (Ankerkrone chandelier by Poul Henningsen, BELOW) and furniture (table and chairs by Poul Kjaerholm, OPPOSITE) liberates them from a solely utilitarian role.

HEARTH AND HOME

In the earliest Nordic houses, the kitchen did not so much have a hearth as it *was* the hearth. Especially during long winters, few ventured more than several feet away from the fireplace, which was the source of heat, fuel for cooking, and light. Often built waist-high and with an extended stone "counter" to accommodate the shuffling of heavy pots and serve as a warm holding area, the hearth was the immovable core of the kitchen to which furniture was drawn near. An enormous hood over the entire hearth drew smoke from the room; below the hearth openings for wood storage were often built in.

Whether it's needed or not in contemporary houses (and it often is, especially in more remote cabins and cottages), few Scandinavians by choice go without a kitchen fireplace. They value the connection to history and nature and treasure the cheer, warmth, scent, and glow every bit as much as, if not more than, their ancestors.

Fireplaces modeled on historical hearths (BOTTOM AND SECOND FROM BOTTOM) appear in reduced size if not stature in many a Scandinavian kitchen (TOP, SECOND FROM TOP, CENTER, AND RIGHT).

OPPOSITES ATTRACT

The more rustic the house, the more drama installing a truly modern kitchen will deliver. Contrasting
natural and industrial materials is particularly effective. Set in a Swedish cabin with rough-hewn beams
and exposed rafters, an all-stainless-steel cabinet,
incorporating sink and stove, shimmers like a stunning jewel. A single steel rod, a minimal update of
open storage, keeps implements and cups close at
hand. In this setting, traditional cobalt blue for the
window trim takes on a more avant-garde, Yves
Klein aspect.

SEE AND BE SEEN

Scandinavian kitchens, more than most, feature open storage, in the form of shelving, doorless cabinets, and plate racks. Pragmatically, open storage facilitates visual organization and saves time and effort, eliminating the hunt through cupboards and drawers.

But ease counts for little without an overriding aesthetic sense. The selectivity and appreciation of craft, form, and color that Scandinavians bring to the objects they acquire serves them well throughout the house but especially in the kitchen. Neither sterile laboratory nor chaotic cook's corner, the Nordic kitchen is populated with interesting and useful objects sensibly arranged, making the room itself a draw for more than its delicious output.

LEFT In a Norwegian country kitchen otherwise given over to natural wood, a band of open shelving painted cornflower blue visually unites an array of tableware while highlighting the form and color of individual pieces.

OVERLEAF, LEFT Above graceful serving pieces gathered on a demilune table, a row of simple pegs features everyday objects with graphic appeal.

OVERLEAF, TOP RIGHT The warm slate gray chosen for a kitchen in Norway beautifully complements both dark and light tableware.

OVERLEAF, BOTTOM RIGHT Here the open shelving acts as a decorative and functional screen dividing the kitchen and dining areas.

SOFT SWEDISH HUES

Extending a precious resource—natural light—has long guided the Swedes in their choice of interior colors for every room in the house, kitchens included. The pale, French-influenced colors favored in the Rococo and Gustavian periods of the eighteenth century comprise the palette still most associated with Sweden. Warm hues like soft yellows and pinks balance the cool northern light. Other shades, like an array of pearly grays, pale blues, and whites, carry on its clean character. As free as they are with paint, though, Scandinavians tend to leave pine board floors in the kitchen in their natural state, maintaining a light, almost pickled effect, with occasional sanding and regular scrubbing.

OPPOSITE Curtains in a traditional bold navy-and-white check spike the otherwise soft blue of a kitchen in Sweden.

TOP White unites the wood-lined surfaces and disparate furnishings of this kitchen in the Swedish countryside.

BOTTOM In the kitchen at Regnaholm, a straw-colored band wrapping the walls warms the atmosphere of the room and reduces its grand proportions to a more intimate scale.

The natural straw color that forms the high dado in the kitchen of Regnaholm manor house is original to the eighteenth century, as is the band of battleship gray paint that acts as a visual baseboard.

NORWAY'S STRONG SHADES

Kitchens in Norway are, colorwise, some of the boldest in Scandinavia, a visual reflection of a strong and adventurous spirit dating back to the Vikings. The saturated primary colors often used are rooted in its tradition of folk painting, which, by necessity, drew on a palette comprised of readily available pigments: a barn red and ochre yellow, derived from iron oxide, and cobalt blue, a byproduct of copper mining. The strong colors have the effect of making Norway's generally intimate kitchens simultaneously striking and cozy.

TOP AND OPPOSITE Brilliant white trim crisply sets off the intense blue and rich red of the painted wood walls in two Norwegian kitchens. A connecting pantry exhibits a soft gray green that balances the red while matching its value.

BOTTOM Golden yellow walls echo the warmth of the fire and brighten a fairly dark country kitchen.

BATHROOMS

Given to underindulgence, Scandinavians view their bathrooms much as others view laundry rooms—as a place for getting something done. In their homes, a fantasy spa bath would be as out of place as a tricked-out screening room. Yet, in their simplicity and intelligent use of materials, Nordic bathrooms have great charm and can be especially striking in contemporary houses.

In the predominantly rural landscape of Scandinavia, bathrooms came inside only in the latter part of the nineteenth century and privies dot the countryside to this day. By choice, many a Finn still eschews indoor plumbing for his weekend or vacation house, preferring the contact with nature imposed by outhouses and lake bathing. In Scandinavian bathrooms, "nature calls" takes on more than one meaning. Especially in log country cabins and wood lakeside houses, leaving the natural timber exposed maintains a seamless link to the outdoors. Moreover, an all-wood bathroom takes the chill out of stripping down, its warm tones an antidote to cool porcelain fixtures. Even in such a private room, window coverings are rare, facilitated by the relative isolation of most country houses and a culture far more comfortable with nudity than most.

The Scandinavian lack of self-consciousness when it comes to the body and bathing is rooted in the sauna, itself a tradition as old as the Vikings, though now most often associated with the Finns. With 187,888 lakes larger than 500 square meters (nearly 5,400 square feet) and 95,000 coastal islands, Finland provides an ideal setting for saunas: plenty of woods for shelter and building materials and easy proximity to water for an invigorating post-sauna plunge. In a land that boasts two million saunas for just five million people, 95 percent of children have experienced, by the age of two, the delightful warmth and freedom of their first sauna, and benefited, though they of all people need it least, from its purification.

Though secreted in an apartment in Stockholm, a serenely spare bathroom designed by the Swedish architecture firm Claesson Koivisto Rune summons the feeling of bathing outdoors under a full moon.

ESCAPE TO THE WOODS

Woodsy bathrooms extend the feeling of being close to nature. In a Swedish bathroom, the only elements that aren't wood are the tile floor and ceramic sink, set into a simple country dresser (LEFT). A bathroom made cozier by the addition of a few antiques retains the soft contours of log walls (RIGHT). Decorating crosses cultures and periods in a bathroom where classical plaster medallions, a French wood-handled bucket, and a polycarbonate Louis Ghost chair by Philippe Starck add flair (BELOW LEFT). In a vibrantly blue, well-furnished outhouse, only the toilet seat and floor remain in their natural wood state (BELOW RIGHT).

DRESSED UP

Though utilitarian by nature, a bathroom can be as inviting as a sitting room. Furnishing it with chairs, dressers, decorative sconces, and unusual bathroom fixtures softens its clinical image. Curtains and pretty upholstery fabrics add a layer of warmth and comfort particularly welcome in cool northern climates, just as introducing deeper hues creates an environment that feels clubby and snug.

BELOW LEFT In a bathroom warmed by a Norwegian iron stove, an exceptional steel sink surround incorporating a skirted base with graceful cabriole legs and a beveled oval mirror turns mundane daily ablutions into an event.

BELOW RIGHT Plaid wool curtains, a folkloric side chair, and moldings painted to resemble burled wood together project a sophisticated masculine air. Against the dark slate tile floor, the white sink stands out as an even more pristine vessel.

OPPOSITE The master bath in Lars Bolander's country house in Sweden is not easily identified as such, given the abundance of decorative flourishes like an antique French carved floral candle sconce, a pair of Gustavian chairs, prints in gilded frames, a bust of Gustav III, and a marble sandal-clad foot resting atop a tub encased in faux marble. The stairway leads to the master bedroom.

PURE AND CLEAN

In the modern Scandinavian bathroom bathing is reduced to its essence with all extraneous details, flourishes, and functions washed away. Planes of modern materials lend strong form to splendidly plain rooms. Nature gives life to the rooms through expanses of glass that admit shifting light and frame ever-changing color.

OPPOSITE In an otherwise all-white bathroom, a deeply stained wood wall is powerful both graphically and historically, in its reference to early wood houses sealed with tar.

TOP Sheets of frosted glass are elegant yet practical solutions to two different needs: as an angled "curtain" for a shower tucked in a corner and as a door to a connecting sauna.

BOTTOM Defined by two walls of glass, the shower in this Swedish bathroom captures the feel of bathing outdoors year round.

THE SAUNA

The only Finnish noun known the world over, *sauna* represents health via heat. Though city saunas are by necessity mostly electric, countryside saunas are wood-fired, heating coarse stones like peridotite to a dry and very tolerable 140–210° F (60–99° C). Partakers can self-regulate the temperature by selecting between upper (hotter) and lower (cooler) benches and using a towel to shield parts of the body, particularly the head. Splashing water on the heated rocks produces a burst of steam, encouraging cleansing perspiration. The circulatory benefits of swatting and being swatted with a *vasta* (young leafy silver birch branches tied together) are so appreciated that tender branches are cut in the spring and frozen for later use.

TOP Contemporary saunas often feature benches of ribbed wood for superior comfort and circulation.

BOTTOM A wooden chair provides another temperature option in a rustic Finnish sauna.

RIGHT A wood bucket and dipper, a *vasta* of birch branches, and a wooden ladder towel rack furnish a classic Finnish sauna.

BEDROOMS

For centuries the design of bedrooms in Scandinavia centered on one thing only: keeping warm. The earliest farmhouse bedrooms were not rooms at all but simply areas near the hearth within a large room that accommodated working, cooking, and eating as well as sleeping. For the sake of warmth as well as privacy (and protection from ash and smoke), the bed area increasingly came to be defined as an intimate room within a room. That meant either tucking the bed into a corner or alcove, constructing a framework around the bed, or a combination of the two.

Even in modest farmhouses, the most significant piece of furniture in the household was often an impressive bedstead, the elaborate carved structure and painting of which conveyed the stature of the family. Because of its strong heritage of shipbuilding and folk art, particularly *rosemaling,* or rose painting (see pages 76–77), Norway produced especially grand, bold, and colorful box beds and cupboard beds that provided both enclosure and storage. A less-acknowledged Norwegian contribution to bed craft is a design that incorporates multiple slats to support a mattress, a construction that can be traced all the way back to the tenth century, when Vikings used such techniques to fabricate strong yet collapsible furniture easily stowed on ships.

Beds in Sweden have historically been lighter in style, lending an elegant, rather than commanding, presence to a room. The late-eighteenth-century taste for a more classical formality led to a new style of "imperial" bed, modeled after royal French beds, with delicately carved and painted headboards and footboards and side supports that could collapse the bed to half its normal length in order to free up space in the room. Similarly, one model of a single daybed could double in size when its long side was pulled out.

Even in elegant manor houses like that at Regnaholm, the beds were simple painted pine four-posters with pleasing proportions. The leafy shade of green was heavily favored in the mid-eighteenth century, especially for tiled stoves just coming into vogue.

TEXTILES

For centuries, Nordic textiles were largely practical in use and subtle in design, and always all natural: Rya wool rugs and blankets, runners woven of worn cloth, plain muslin curtains, bed linens in simple florals such as the Ekebyholm pattern (LEFT), hard-wearing linen and cotton cushion covers, often in checks (TOP ROW LEFT), table linens in traditional stripes and small patterns (BOTTOM ROW CENTER), like those still made by Ekelund weavers, a Swedish company established in 1692. But the textiles most associated with Scandinavia are hardly the retiring types. The postwar period witnessed a graphic revolution with the punch delivered by two key players: Josef Frank for Svenskt Tenn of Sweden and Marimekko of Finland.

The bold patterns and bright colors of Marimekko's printed cottons—Kaivo (MIDDLE ROW CENTER) and Joonas (BOTTOM ROW LEFT)—were at first radical and soon ubiquitous in modern interiors of the 1960s and 1970s. Patterns like Unikko (MIDDLE ROW RIGHT), a striking floral designed by Maija Isola in 1964, were Pop Art democratized in fabric, the yardage as likely to be framed as thrown over a table or sofa.

Though the designs of Josef Frank never achieved the global popularity of Marimekko, the dozens of patterns he produced, many of which are still available—Marble (TOP ROW RIGHT), Hawaii (MIDDLE ROW LEFT), Poisons (BOTTOM ROW RIGHT)—are equally dramatic in scale, more complex in coloration, delightfully inventive, and unexpectedly exotic. A native Austrian turned adoptive Swede, Frank displayed an imagination remarkably wild and free-associating for his time, presaging the 1960s with designs that could have illustrated the then-unfamiliar term *psychedelic*.

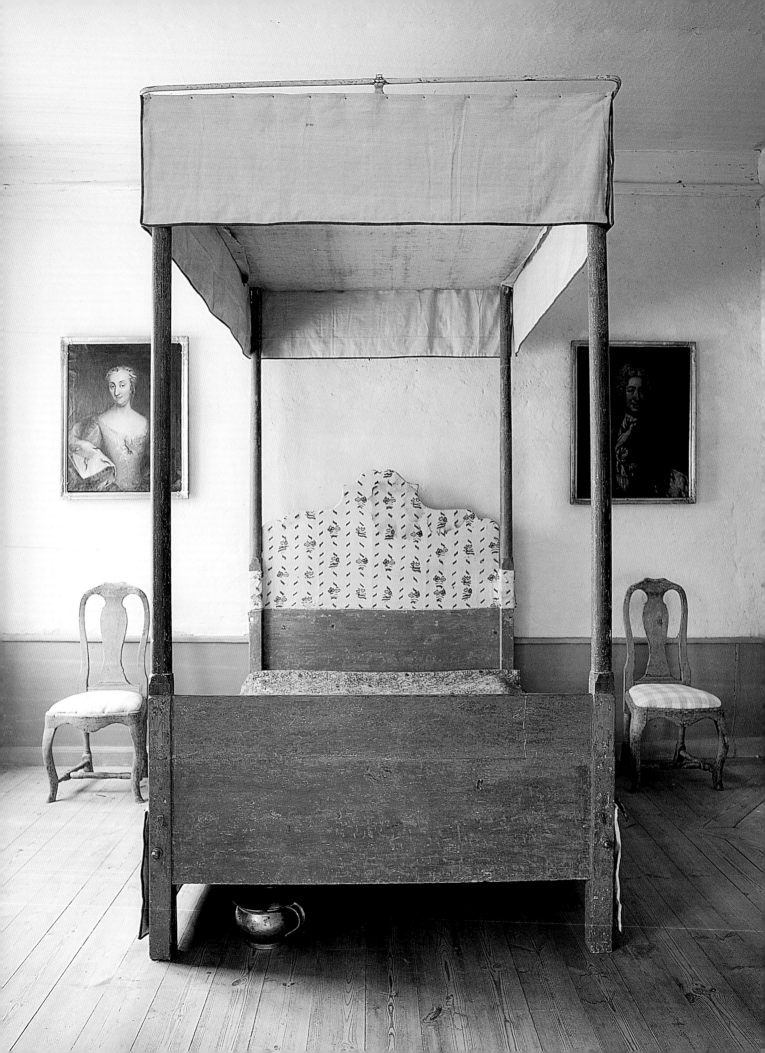

OUT IN THE OPEN

With the widespread adoption of tiled stoves in the late eighteenth century, bedsteads moved out from corners, shed their heavy drapery, and took up positions mid-wall for a pleasing symmetry. Altogether airier, slender posts of canopy beds supported now purely decorative bed hangings in cotton solids, stripes, and prints. A new Gustavian style of bed, inspired by French beds in royal châteaux, itself displayed symmetry, allowing it to function as a sofa by day. Raised on delicate feet, its more formal neoclassical detailing often included fluting and beading, corners embellished with finials, a decorative flourish such as a crown, urn, or wreath midway along the back, and a half-tester above. Beds with crested testers known as *lit à la polonaise*, were also popular.

OPPOSITE A rich yellow dado rings a bedroom in Regnaholm, furnished with a pair of Rococo side chairs and bedstead in their original soft green paint.

TOP Gilding and silk drapery rarely appear in Scandinavia in other than royal residences like this bedroom at Svartå manor house in Finland.

BOTTOM The eighteenth-century taste for all things classical is clear in this bedroom in Regnaholm, where engravings encircle a fine mahogany daybed.

TUCKED IN

Nothing is as cozy as a sheltered bed. With modern heating, an enclosed bed is no longer requisite. Yet its charm holds, so much so that beds curtained or otherwise sheltered by an alcove or under the eaves are still commonly found, even preferred.

Box beds (OPPOSITE, TOP LEFT AND RIGHT), cupboard beds (OPPOSITE, BOTTOM LEFT), and beds in alcoves (BELOW) were originally, by necessity, shelters from the cold. But the appeal of enclosure endures, as a modern children's bedroom (OPPOSITE, BOTTOM RIGHT) demonstrates.

UNDER THE EAVES

With second-story farmhouse bedrooms often lacking in headroom, Scandinavians make the most of limited space by tucking beds against the wall, putting the slope of the ceiling to work as a canopy. The addition of sheepskins (LEFT), checked curtains (TOP), and a simple cotton canopy (BOTTOM) creates an even cozier nest. In particularly close spaces, installing a tiny window or a skylight relieves any claustrophobia.

OVERLEAF In two bedrooms nestled under the roof, a metal bedstead is positioned to capture the view through a dormer (LEFT) and a striped blanket mimics the ribs of the wood ceiling and the simple stanchions of a railing (RIGHT).

BRIGHT IDEAS

Ever conscious of maximizing space and utility, Nordic designers extend the bedroom's function by incorporating sitting areas and home offices into sleep spaces. Windows reduced to rhythmic slots (LEFT) temper the midnight sun in an all-white bedroom. Like an iceberg split in two, a pair of lounge chairs complements the strong form of the hooded fireplace. In another contemporary bedroom furnished with a sculptural fireplace (BELOW), a wall of cupboards accommodates a variety of needs, freeing the room to shift roles at the pull of a handle. Even in the most modern of houses, a fireplace remains a focal point and a connection to the past.

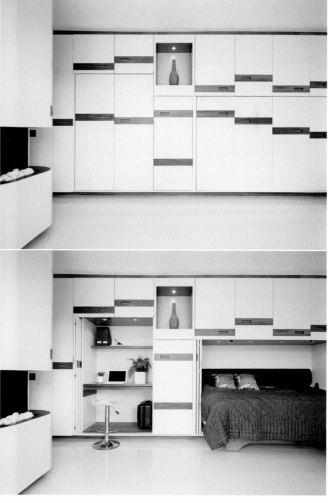

LIGHTING

Scandinavians are so enamored of natural light in all its shades and qualities that if they could, they would dispense with artificial lighting altogether. But winters are long and candles go only so far. As with furniture, lighting in the mid-twentieth century experienced an explosion of imagination and innovation. And as with furniture, Danes trained in architecture led the way as designers. Poul Henningsen in particular experimented with materials and form to produce fixtures radical in design, optimal in illumination, and sensitive to the human eye. His pioneering lights such as the Artichoke, 1958 (MIDDLE ROW CENTER), and the PH3 family of fixtures, 1926, ranging from pendants (BELOW AND BOTTOM ROW RIGHT) to sconces to floor and table lamps (TOP ROW RIGHT), are the result of his dedicated exploration of reflectors to distribute light in multiple directions and of varying finishes to deliver different qualities of light, depending on the setting (warmer for domestic, cooler for institutional). If, as Henningsen professed, "it is an art to make light both economical and glare free," then he was nothing less than the master.

Like the seventy-two overlapping leaves of Henningsen's Artichoke fixture, staggered ribs of "peel" gathered top and bottom form another iconic pendant delivering diffuse light—the Onion fixture (MIDDLE ROW RIGHT) by designer Verner Panton. Even his VP Globe, 1970 (BOTTOM ROW CENTER), plays with lacquered-aluminum reflectors to direct light, although they are encased in a bubble of acrylic, a mod (at the time) material. Architect-designers Arne Jacobsen, Alvar Aalto, and Jørgen Wolf opted for strong, simple forms emitting unidirectional light in the AJ Table Light, 1956

(BOTTOM ROW LEFT); the Kultakello, 1937, here in white (TOP ROW LEFT); and a conical pendant in Oregon pine, 1957 (MIDDLE ROW LEFT), respectively. Poul Christiansen's designs liberated the straight lines of traditional pleated shades; his Le Klint Pendant 172 (TOP ROW CENTER), perhaps the most sinuous—and certainly the best known—of his sculptural lamps for manufacturer Le Klint, required skillful hand folding along geometrically conceived lines. With their preference for pendant fixtures, a form that dominates Nordic lighting design, Scandinavians seem to be ensuring that, no matter how long the stretches of darkness, they will never be without the orbs of the sun or the full moon.

PORCELAIN DREAMS

The calm palette of blue and white takes a bold turn in a Stockholm
bedroom. Though layering pattern is rare in contemporary Scandinavian decorating, the partnering of an overscale wall covering with
a decoratively tiled stove succeeds because the two share a common
coloration and graphic flourish. Against the profusion of pattern, a bed
dressed in plain white linens is a sleep-inducing oasis of calm.

THE BOLANDER LOOK

A Lars Bolander bedroom is unmistakably Swedish yet always cosmopolitan. Mixed in with traditional checked curtains and Gustavian chairs and benches are headboards comfortably upholstered (TOP) or fashioned in seventeenth-century French style (ABOVE), sisal matting, and bold strokes of neoclassicism (RIGHT) in the form of oversize urns and busts.

CENTERED AND SERENE

Whether in a spare contemporary bedroom (ABOVE) or a warm and woodsy bedroom at Salaholm manor house (OPPOSITE), a bed placed in the middle of the space establishes an equanimity that enhances rest.

SOURCES

SCANDINAVIA/EUROPE

Artek Helsinki
Eteläesplanadi 18
00130 Helsinki, Finland
+358 (0)9 6132 5277
www.artek.fi
*Authorized Alvar Aalto
reproductions*

Asplund
Sibyllegatan 31
114 42 Stockholm, Sweden
+46(0)8 662 52 84
www.asplund.org
*Contemporary Swedish
furniture and rugs*

Blås & Knåda
Hornsgatan 26
118 20 Stockholm, Sweden
+46(0)8 642 77 67
www.blasknada.com
*Contemporary Swedish glass
and ceramics*

Dansk Møbelkunst
Bredgade 32
1260 Copenhagen, Denmark
+45 33 323 837
Galerie Dansk Møbelkunst
53 bis, Quai des Grands
Augustins
75006 Paris, France
+33 (1) 4325 1165
www.dmk.dk
*Scandinavian furniture 1920–
1975, emphasis on Danish
Modern*

Design House Stockholm
Smålandsgatan 11
111 56 Stockholm, Sweden
+46(0)8 509 08 113
www.designhousestockholm
.com
*Modern and useful Nordic
furniture and objects*

Ekelund
Varbergsvägen 442
519 30 Horred, Sweden
+46(0)32 020 90 00
www.ekelundweavers.com
*Traditional and
contemporary Swedish textiles*

Finsk Form
Stortorget 21
211 34 Malmö, Sweden
+46(0)4 023 02 01
www.finskform.se
*Finnish design and fashion in
Malmö*

Gallerie Grefmar
Regementsgatan 14
211 42 Malmö, Sweden
+46(0)4 030 23 36
www.studiocarinagrefmar.se
*20th-century Scandinavian
and European furniture,
lighting, and arts and crafts*

Galleri Stolen
Spårvägshallarna
Birger Jarlsgatan 57
113 56 Stockholm, Sweden
+46(0)8 442 91 50
www.galleristolen.se
*Contemporary Swedish
furniture*

Gärsnäs
Rödbodtorget 2
111 52 Stockholm, Sweden
+46(0)8 442 91 50
garsnas.se
*Contemporary Swedish
furniture*

Georg Jensen
Amagertorv 4
1160 Copenhagen, Denmark
+45 33 114 080
www.georgjensen.com
*Best selection of Danish
master of silver*

**Gudrum Odman
Antikhandel**
Grev Turegatan 45
114 38 Stockholm, Sweden
+46(0)8 660 78 51
www.gudrunodmann.com
*Swedish antiques, emphasis
on Gustavian period*

Histoire
Turfstraat 7a
6811 HL Arnhem,
Netherlands
+31(0)26 370 90 80
www.histoire.nl
*Scandinavian mid-century
Modern*

IKEA
Multiple locations
www.ikea.com
*Affordable, Swedish-inspired
home furnishings and fixtures*

Iittala
Pohjoisesplanadi 25
00100 Helsinki, Finland
+358 (0)2 0439-3501
www.iittala.com
*Finland's most notable
producer of glass*

Jackson Design AB
Sibyllegatan 53
114 43 Stockholm, Sweden
+46(0)8 665 33 50

Jacksons
Lindenstrasse 34
10969 Berlin, Germany
+49 30 505 99 777
www.jacksons.se
*Specialists in Scandinavian
design 1880–1980*

**Klassik Moderne
Møbelkunst**
Bredgade 3, Nyhavn
1260 Copenhagen, Denmark
+45 33 339 060
www.klassik.dk
*Scandinavian design
(furniture, lighting, objects)
1920–1975*

Le Klint
Store Kirkestræde 1
1073 Copenhagen, Denmark
+45 33 116 663
www.leklint.dk
*Specialists in folded pendant
lights*

**Lars Edelstam Konst &
Antikviteter**
Linnégatan 26
114 47 Stockholm, Sweden
+46(0)8 611 49 80
www.edelstam-antik.se
*Emphasis on Gustavian
furniture and Swedish
decorative objects*

Ljungbergs
Fabriksvägen 4
515 70 Rydboholm, Sweden
+46(0)3 023 71 70
www.ljungbergstextil.se
*Traditional and
contemporary Swedish textiles*

Louis Poulsen
Gammel Strand 28
1202 Copenhagen, Denmark
+45 70 331 414
www.louispoulsen.com
*Leading Danish lighting
manufacturer*

Malmsten
Strandvägen 5b
114 51 Stockholm, Sweden
+46(0)8 23 33 80
www.malmsten.se
*Classic designs of Carl
Malmsten and contemporary
designers*

Marimekko
Multiple locations
www.marimekko.fi
Fabric, furnishings, and clothing from Finland's brightest textile company

Möbel-Shop Sven Larsson
Renstiernasg 24
111 52 Stockholm, Sweden
+46(0)8 644 40 00
Södergatan 7
211 34 Malmö, Sweden
+46(0)4 023 83 45
Kungsgatan 4
411 19 Göteborg, Sweden
+46(0)3 113 36 52
www.mobelshop.com
Contemporary furniture by Larsson and others

Modernity
Sibyllegatan 6
114 42 Stockholm, Sweden
+46(0)8 20 80 25
www.modernity.se
Vintage 20th-century furnishings, emphasis on Scandinavian

Nordiska Galleriet
Nybrogatan 11
111 52 Stockholm, Sweden
+46(0)8 442 83 60
www.nordiskagalleriet.se
Classic contemporary furniture

Norrgavel
Birger Jarlsgatan 27
Stockholm, Sweden
Magasinsgatan 22
411 18 Göteborg, Sweden
Engelbrektsgatan 20
211 33 Malmö, Sweden
www.norrgavel.se
Home furnishings in a Swedish/Shaker vein

Orrefors + Kosta Boda
Birger Jarlsgatan 15
111 45 Stockholm, Sweden
+46(0)8 545 040 84
www.kostaboda.se
www.orrefors.se
Leading Swedish producers of crystal and glass

Retro Modern Design
Kopparmöllegatan 19
254 35 Helsingborg, Sweden
+46(0)4 214 27 70
www.retromoderndesign.com
Mid-century Scandinavian design

Scandinavian Design Online
Slöjdaregatan 1
393 53 Kalmar, Sweden
www.scandinaviandesigncenter.com
All things Scandinavian, from carpets to candleholders

Starkeld of Scandinavia
Lars Andreasson
Kurirgatan 13
254 53 Helsingborg, Sweden
www.starkeld.com
Vintage Scandinavian art pottery

Stockholm Modern
Karlavägen 26
Stockholm, Sweden
+46(0)8 10 14 13
20th-century design

Svensk Slöjd
Nybrogatan 23
114 39 Stockholm, Sweden
+46(0)8 663 66 50
www.svenskslojd.se
Traditional Sami handicrafts

Svenskt Tenn
Strandvägen 5
Stockholm, Sweden
+46(0)8 670 16 00
www.svenskttenn.se
Home of the Swedish Modern aesthetic, Josef Frank reproductions

Tomorrow's Antique
Runeberginkatu 35
00100 Helsinki, Finland
+358 5 064 320
www.tomorrowsantique.com
Finnish furniture and lighting 1930–1980

VerPan
Egeskovvej 29
8700 Horsens, Denmark
+45 76 581 882
www.verpan.dk
Lighting designs by Verner Panton and contemporary designers

BoConcept
Multiple locations
www.boconcept.co.uk
Danish retail furniture chain

Fragile Design
14-15 The Custard Factory
Digbeth, Birmingham
B9 4AA, UK
+44 (0)121 224 7378
www.fragiledesign.com
Vintage 20th-century design for the home

The Modern Warehouse
243B Victoria Park Road
Hackney
London E9 7HD, UK
+44 (0)20 89860740
www.themodernwarehouse.com
Original vintage furniture and accessories from Scandinavia and beyond

Pure Imagination
2 Westoe Village
South Shields
NE33 3DZ, UK
+44 (0)771 5054919
www.vintageretro.co.uk
20th-century furniture from Scandinavia

Skandium
247 Brompton Road
London SW3 2EP, UK
+44 (0)20 7584 2066
www.skandium.com
Scandinavian design classics

A. Tyner Antiques
200 Bennett Street N.W.
Atlanta, GA 30309
404 367-4484
www.swedishantiques.biz
18th- and 19th-century Swedish furniture, especially clocks and demilune tables

Antik
104 Franklin St.
New York, NY 10013
212 343-0471
www.antik-nyc.net
20th-century furniture and ceramics

Arenskjold
605 Warren St.
Hudson, NY 12534
518 828-2800
www.arenskjold.com
Antiques with a focus on Danish Modern, mid-century furniture

Avolli, LLC
P.O. Box 2607
South Portland, ME 04116
207 767-1901
3 Southgate Road,
Suite 1 and 2
Scarborough, ME 04074
207 767-1901
www.avolli.com
Swedish antiques in the Gustavian, Biedermeier, Art Deco, and Mid-century Modern styles

Birgit Antiques
608½ Warren St.
Hudson, NY 12534
518 828-1944
www.birgitantiques.com
Focus on Scandinavian ceramics 1930–1990

Blondell Antiques
Tom and Doris Blondell
1406 2nd Street S.W.
Rochester, MN 55902
507 282-1872
www.blondell.com
Swedish and Norwegian antiques, especially painted furniture

Calico Corners
Multiple locations
www.calicocorners.com
*Retailers of fine fabrics,
many inspired by
Scandinavian patterns*

Choate and von Z.
6635 Paxson Rd.
Solebury, PA 18963
215 784-8695
www.choateandvonz.com
*18th- and 19th-century
Swedish antiques*

Clearly First
980 Madison Avenue
New York, NY 10021
212 988-8242
www.clearlyfirst.com
*Scandinavian furniture,
objects, and clothing*

**The Country Gallery
Antiques**
P.O. Box 70
1566 Route 315
Rupert, VT 05768
802 394-7753
www.country-gallery.com
*Restored antique Scandinavian
pine furniture*

Country Swedish
22 Elizabeth Street
South Norwalk, CT 06854
203 855-1106
979 Third Avenue,
Suite 1409
New York, NY 10022
212 838-1976
1621 Merchandise Mart
Chicago, IL 60654
312 644-4540
www.countryswedish.com
*Reproduction Gustavian
furniture, rugs, wallpaper,
fabric*

**Cupboards & Roses Swedish
Antiques**
296 South Main Street,
Route 7
Sheffield, MA 01257
413 229-3070
www.cupboardsandroses.
com
*18th- and 19th-century
painted Swedish furniture,
Scandinavian folk art*

Danish Country
138 Charles Street
Boston, MA 02114
617 227-1804
www.europeanstyleantiques
.com
*Danish, Swedish, and Asian
Antiques*

Danish Teak Classics
1500 Jackson St. NE,
Suite 277
Minneapolis, MN 55413
612 362-7870
www.danishteakclassics.com
Danish Modern furniture

Dawn Hill Antiques
11 Main Street
New Preston, CT 06777
860 868-0066
www.dawnhillantiques.com
*18th- and 19th-century
Swedish antiques*

Denmark 50
7974 Melrose Ave.
Los Angeles, CA 90046
323 653-9726
www.denmark50.com
*Danish Mid-century Modern
furniture and ceramics*

Dienst & Dotter
23 Bridge Street
Sag Harbor, NY 11963
631 725-6881
www.dienstanddotter.com
*Scandinavian antiques,
paintings, and objects from
the 17th to the mid-20th
century*

Eleish van Breems, Ltd.
18 Titus Road
P.O. Box 313
Washington Depot, CT
06794
860 868-1200
www.evbantiques.com
*18th- and 19th-century
Swedish design, both antique
and reproduction*

Ericson Gallery
P.O. Box 12212
Des Moines, IA 50312
515 279-0591
www.ericsongallery.com
*Unusual Scandinavian folk
art, textiles, and metalware*

Evergreen Antiques
1249 Third Avenue
New York, NY 10021
212 744-5664
www.evergreenantiques.com
*Scandinavian, Northern
European, Russian, and
Baltic Neoclassical Antiques*

FinnStyle
651 Nicollet Mall, Suite 207
Minneapolis, MN 55401
612 333-2127
www.finnstyle.com
*Finnish home furnishings,
clothing, jewelry, and gifts*

Fjorn Scandinavian
877 706-0384
www.fjorn.com
*Online source for
Scandinavian home
furnishings and clothing*

House of Copenhagen
www.houseofcopenhagen
.com
Danish design classics

Huset
1112 Montana Ave., # 334
Santa Monica, CA 90403
310 459-5524
www.huset-shop.com
*Modern Scandinavian
furniture, objects, clothing,
accessories*

Jane Moore Interiors
2922 Virginia Street
Houston, TX 77098
713 526-6113
Swedish antiques

Joli International
7878 Roswell Road, Suite 300
Atlanta, GA 30350
405 259-9148
www.joliinternational.com
*18th- and 19th-century
Swedish furniture, especially
Gustavian and Allmoge*

Just Scandinavian
161 Hudson Street
New York, NY 10013
212 334-2556
www.justscandinavian.com
*Classic Scandinavian modern
furniture, fabric, and objects*

**Karl Kemp & Associates,
Ltd.**
36 East 10th Street
New York, NY 10003
212 254-1877

833 Madison Avenue
New York, NY 10021
212 288-3838
www.karlkemp.com
*Biedermeier and Neoclassical
antiques*

**Klaradal Swedish Antiques
& Furnishings**
16644 Georgia Avenue
Olney, MD 20832
301 570-2557
www.klaradal.com
*Antique Swedish furniture,
new objects, and gifts*

Lars Bolander
72 Gansevoort Street
New York, NY 10014
212 924-1000
3731 South Dixie Highway
West Palm Beach, FL 33405
561 832-2121
www.larsbolander.com
*Focus on Swedish furniture,
fabric, and decorative arts*

The Lenkoran Gallery
675 Sackett St.
Brooklyn, NY 11226
212 655-9352
www.lenkoran.co.uk
*18th- and early-19th-century
Swedish rugs*

Lief, Inc.
646 North Almont Drive
West Hollywood, CA 90069
310 492-0033
www.liefalmont.com
*Swedish furniture, objects,
and paintings, from the
Baroque period to mid-
twentieth century*

Marimekko North America
Multiple locations
www.marimekko.us
*Fabric, furnishings, and
clothing from Finland's
brightest textile company*

Midnight Sun Antiques
110 West Lake Street
Libertyville, IL 60048
847 362-5240
www.midnightsunantiques
.com
*Antique, vintage, and
reproduction Swedish
furniture*

ModernLink
35 Bond St.
New York, NY 10012
212 254-1300
www.modernlink.com
*Vintage Scandinavian design
classics and modern lines*

More North
39 N. Moore St.
New York, NY 10013
212 334-5541
www.morenorth.com
*Classic and contemporary
Scandinavian furniture, fine
art, and crafts*

Next Step Antiques
199 Ethan Allen Highway
(Rt. 7)
Ridgefield, CT 06877
203 431-8083
www.nextstepantiques.com
*Swedish antiques, furniture,
and accessories*

Nordic Style
1005 North Commons Drive
Aurora, IL 60504
630 851-2111
www.nordicstyle.com
*Reproduction Swedish
furniture, fabric, and paint*

Real Gustavian
389 Stockbridge Road
Great Barrington, MA 01230
413 528-4440
www.realgustavian.com
*Antique and reproduction
Gustavian furniture*

Regeneration
38 Renwick St.
New York, NY 10013
212 741-2102
www.regenerationfurniture
.com
*Mid-twentieth-century
vintage furniture, especially
Danish and American*

St. Barths Home
303 Broadway
Suite 104-123
Laguna Beach, CA 92657
800 274-9096
www.stbarthshome.com
*Antique and reproduction
Swedish furniture*

Scandinavian Grace
2866 Route 28
Shokan, NY 12481
845 657-2759
www.scandinaviangrace.com
*Classic and contemporary
Scandinavian design*

Svenska Möbler
154 N. LaBrea Ave.
Los Angeles, CA 90036
323 934-4452
516 N. Wells St.
Chicago, IL 60610
312 595-9320
www.svenskamobler.com
*19th- and 20th-century
Swedish furniture*

Swede Home
P.O. Box 460103
Ft. Lauderdale, FL 33346
954 829-6272
www.swedehomeantiques.net
*Antique and reproduction
Gustavian furniture*

Swedish Blonde
303 Broadway
Laguna Beach, VA 92651
800 274-9096
www.swedishblonde.com
*Reproduction Gustavian
furniture*

Swedish Country Interiors
6016 Alpine Dr. SW
Olympia, WA 98512
360 570-0876
www.swedishcountry.com
*Antique, vintage, and new
Swedish furniture and objects*

Swedish Heirlooms
2911 East Madison Street
Seattle, WA 98112
206 621-1002
www.swedishheirlooms.com
*Reproduction Gustavian
furniture*

Swedish Room
Suzanna Havden Bell
Sobel Design Building
680 Eight Street, Suite 151
San Francisco, CA 94103
415 255-0154
www.swedishroom.com
*Antique and reproduction
Swedish furniture*

Tivoli Home
111 Front Street
Brooklyn, NY 11201
718 666-3050
www.tivolihome.com
*Contemporary Scandinavian
design home furnishings*

Tone on Tone
7920 Woodmont Avenue
Bethesda, MD 20814
240 497-0800
www.tone-on-tone.com
*18th- and 19th-century
painted Swedish antiques*

Vitra
29 Ninth Avenue
New York, NY 10014
212 463-5700
www.vitra.com
*Modern and contemporary
Scandinavian furniture*

White on White
313 Main St.
Great Barrington, MA 01230
413 528-4440
www.whiteonwhiteny.com
*Vintage and reproduction
Swedish furniture*

INDEX

136; open, *132–33*; open
    storage in, *142–45*;
    renovated, *128–29,*
    140–41
Kjaerholm, Poul, 65, 66;
    furniture, *137*; house,
    62–63
Kultakello, *177*
kurbits painting, 76

lacquered furniture, 11
lakes, Finland, 8, 36
lamps, *64*
Landström, Anders, 17
Larsson, Carl: dining room,
    13; *Ett Hem* (A Home),
    12
Le Klint manufacturer, 176
Le Klint Pendant 172, *177*
light, 7–8, 13; amplifying,
    51; in kitchens, 132; not
    obstructing, 60
lighting, *176–77*
Linnaeus, Carl, 12;
    farmhouse. *See*
    Hammarby
Little Alhambra, *24–25*
living rooms, 50–91
log cabins, 8
Louis Ghost chair, *155*
lounge chairs, *67*
Lysøen island, 24

manor houses, *18–19*; colors
    in, 75
Marble pattern, *165*
Marieberg factory, 54, 127
Marimekko textiles, 164–65
medallions, *38, 42, 100–101*
Mies van der Rohe, Ludwig,
    13
minimalism, 13, 51
mirrors, 88
modern style: bedrooms,
    174–75, 182; dining
    rooms, 106; stoves, 54
Moorish arches, 113
Mora, Sweden, 120
Mora clocks, *50, 120–21*
Murman, Hans, 32, 110

nature: houses open to, 60,
    135; influence of, 8–12
neoclassicism, *38,* 180
neo-Viking Dragon Style, *21*
Noormarkku, Finland, 17

Norway, 8
Norwegian Society for Home
    Industry, 12
Nurmesniemi, Antti, chairs,
    62–63

Onion fixture, *177*
open floor plan, 13, *60–61,*
    132–33
open shelving, *142–43, 145*
Orientalist style, 11
outhouses, 153
Ox chair, *62–63*

painted furniture, 65, 100,
    104–5
painted interiors, *38, 84–87,*
    98–99, 150–51; two-
    tone, 72
panels, linen, 84
Panton, Verner, 66, 176
Panton Chair, *67*
Papa Bear chair, *67*
Peacock Chair, *67*
pewter, 127, 130
PH3 light fixtures, *176–77*
PH5 light fixture, *106*
picnics, *122–25*
pine-tar preservative, 8
pink, 147
PK9 chair, *65*
PK20 chair, *67*
PK22 chair, *67*
PK54 table, *65*
plaster medallions, *38, 42*
plate racks, *130–31, 143*
plates, pewter, 127
Poisons pattern, *165*
Pop Art, 164
porcelain, imported, 11, 127,
    130
porches, 24; for outdoor
    dining, *124–25*
Puotila, Ritva, 113

red, 71, 94; barn, 150; Falun,
    22–23
Regnaholm manor house, 84,
    96–99; bedrooms, *162,*
    166, 167; kitchen, 127,
    147–49
Renaissance Revival, 93, 97
revival styles, 113
Rococo style, 84, 119, 147;
    furniture, 11, *41,* 120,
    166; Swedish, 53, 97

Rörstrand factory, 11, 127
rosemaling, 76, 163
Royal Danish Academy of
    Fine Arts, 66
royal houses, 56
rugs, *40, 64,* 164
Russian style, 24
Rya wool rugs, 164

St. Lucia festival, 7
Salaholm manor house,
    183
saunas, 153, *160–61*
Scandinavian design, main
    features of, 7–13
Scandinavian Modern, 66
scarlet, 75
sconces, 109
Shell Chair, *67*
shelving, *142–43, 145*
Sheraton, *100–101*
showers, *159*
sideboards, *101, 126*
side chair, Rococo, *41, 166*
sink, steel, *156*
sisal matting, 65, 180
Skåne region, Sweden, 10
Skinnarbol manor house, *91*
skylights, 60
sod roofs, *26–27*
spatter-painted wall, *38*
stairways, *39–49, 48–49*
Starck, Philippe, 155
steel, *62–63,* 65, *156*
storehouses, Norwegian,
    26–27
stoves: cast-iron, 54; modern,
    54; wood, *54–55*
Strömstad, Sweden, 17
Svartå manor house, 79;
    bedroom, *167*
Svartsjö hunting lodge, 45,
    46–47
Svenskt Tenn, 164
Sweden, 10–12
Swedish East India
    Company, 11, 81, 130
Swedish Handicraft Society,
    12
Swedish Rococo, 53, 97
symmetry, in Swedish design,
    56, 114

tables: demilune, *144;*
    Empire, *40;* kitchen, 127,
    137

tableware, 127; chinoiserie,
    11; wood, metal, and
    porcelain, 130
tapestry, imitation, *102–3*
teak, 13, 62, 65
terra-cotta color, 71
textile patterns, *164–65*
Tham & Videgård Hansson,
    house by, *14*
Thureholm: chinoiserie at,
    80–81, 83; kitchen at, *9,*
    11, 127
tiled stove (*kakelugn*), 54
trompe l'oeil, 11, *58–59,* 79
tubular steel furniture, *62–63*
two-tone painted walls, 72

Unikko pattern, *165*

Venetian style, 24, 113
Versailles, 12, 56
Vikings, 11, 93, 150, 153, 163
Villa Mairea, *17, 69*
Vodder, Niels, 66
VP Globe, *177*

wallpapers, *84–87,* 119
walls: painted chinoiserie,
    116–17; painted tapestry
    and faux marbling,
    98–99; painted wood,
    150–51; spatter-painted,
    38; two-tone, 72; white,
    60
water, views of, 31, 36
Wegner, Hans, 13, 62, 66
white, 60, 100, 116, 147
wicker, 24
windows, 135; thermal, 60
Wingårdh, Gert and Karin,
    28, 36, 93
Wishbone chair, *62–63*
Wolf, Jørgen, 176
wood, 13; in bathrooms,
    154–55; exteriors, *15–19*
woodcraft, interior, *112–13*
wood stoves, *54–55*
work table, 127
WRB Architects, 135

yellow, 72, 147; golden,
    150–51; ochre, 72, 150;
    straw, 149

PHOTO CREDITS

ACKNOWLEDGMENTS

Never did I think I would enjoy a project as much as I have working on this book. I have met new people who have become great friends, I have been to places that I never would have had occasion to visit, and it has opened my eyes even further to both the architecture and design of the Scandinavian countries.

None of this would have been possible without the help of Jackie Decter and Mark Magowan at Vendome Press, and Heather MacIsaac, who has done an extraordinary job capturing the essence of the Scandinavian aesthetic in her text.

Nor could I ever have dreamed of having a better contact in Copenhagen than Per Arnoldi, now a most valued friend. In Stockholm, as always, there are my two closest and oldest friends, Charlotte Bonnier and Anna Lallerstedt, to whom I am deeply thankful for their willingness to share all of their knowledge with me.

Lars Bolander

To Lars, a most discerning and affable Swede
To Mark, a publisher with wonderfully democratic curiosity and true savoir faire
To Jackie, an editor of such sharp eye, fine ear, and good nature
To Ivy and Cole, my treasures

Heather Smith MacIsaac

ABOVE *A pair of seventeenth-century Swedish chairs repainted a smoky royal blue flank a bust of Queen Christina poised before an eighteenth-century Danish mirror in Lars Bolander's house.*

PAGE 1 *Bold splashes of color—an orange Mora clock and a fauteuil upholstered in a bright plaid—strike a modern note in an eighteenth-century Copenhagen apartment.*

PAGES 2–3 *In a loft at the top of a building in Stockholm, daylight streams in through windows, dormers, and skylights.*

PAGE 191 *Form and palette create a look that's Scandinavian even if the elements—carved wooden animal heads from South America, iron garden chairs from Spain, a pedestal table glazed gray—are not.*

First published in the United States of America in 2010 by
The Vendome Press
1334 York Avenue
New York, NY 10021
www.vendomepress.com

Copyright © 2010 The Vendome Press

ISBN 978-0-86565-258-3

Editor: Jacqueline Decter
Photo Editor: Sarah Davis
Production Editor: Tiffany Hu
Designers: Joel Avirom and Jason Snyder

Library of Congress Cataloging-in-Publication Data

MacIsaac, Heather Smith.
Lars Bolander's Scandinavian design / by Heather Smith MacIsaac.
p. cm.
Includes index.
ISBN 978-0-86565-258-3
1. Design—Scandinavia. 2. Interior decoration—Scandinavia.
I. Bolander, Lars. II. Title. III. Title: Scandinavian design.
NK1457.M33 2010
747.0948—dc22
2009051241

Printed by Toppan Printing Co., Ltd, in China
First printing